P.

10:17am   23 MAY 2003
COQUITLAM PUBLIC LIBRARY RECEIPT
                CHECKOUT

22416001524448

  1) Who gets in : what's wrong wi
32416003837135
DUE 13 JUN 2003

PORT # pofines

M W
&
R

WHO GETS IN

WHO GETS IN

**What's Wrong with Canada's Immigration
Program – and How to Fix It**

DANIEL STOFFMAN

Macfarlane Walter & Ross
Toronto

Macfarlane Walter & Ross
An Affiliate of McClelland & Stewart Ltd.
37A Hazelton Avenue
Toronto, Canada M5R 2E3
www.mwandr.com

National Library of Canada Cataloguing in Publication

Stoffman, Daniel
Who gets in : what's wrong with Canada's immigration program,
and how to fix it / Daniel Stoffman.

Includes bibliographical references and index.
ISBN 1-55199-095-4

1. Canada – Emigration and immigration – Government policy.
I. Title.

JV7233.S76 2002   325.71   C2002-902828-0

Macfarlane Walter & Ross gratefully acknowledges support for its
publishing program from the Canada Council for the Arts, the Ontario
Arts Council, and the Government of Canada through the Book
Publishing Industry Development Program.

Printed and bound in Canada

This book is printed on acid-free paper that is
100% ancient-forest-friendly (100% post-consumer recycled).

CONTENTS

ACKNOWLEDGMENTS

My interest in the subject of immigration goes back to 1991, when I received an Atkinson Fellowship in Public Policy from the Atkinson Charitable Foundation. This unique program each year allows a journalist the luxury of probing deeply enough into a public policy subject to produce a series of major articles that analyze as well as report. Thanks to the Atkinson Fellowship, I was able to spend a year immersed in immigration policy and have continued to study this fascinating subject ever since.

As I researched this book, many people generously shared their knowledge and ideas with me. Many are named in the book; some could not be. I owe a debt of gratitude to them all.

I thank David Foot for reading and commenting on chapter 5, Gerald Bierling for his statistical assistance, and Charles Campbell for alerting me to the work of Lee Gunderson on language learning in Vancouver schools. Of course, no one who contributed their thoughts or ideas bears responsibility for anything in the book. I take full responsibility for that myself.

Thanks are owed to Gary Ross, who embraced the idea for a book on immigration and provided his usual editorial insight, and to Barbara Czarnecki, who scoured the manuscript for inconsistencies and infelicities. As always, my in-house editor, Judy Stoffman, was a source of precious advice and support.

Daniel Stoffman
Toronto, June 2002

INTRODUCTION

IT'S A SWELTERING SUMMER DAY AND THE CLANGING OF THE handbell grows louder as the knife sharpener approaches my house. Soon he's outside my door and the tempo of the ringing picks up. The old man, hopeful of business, has stopped. Sometimes he trudges for blocks without any action, but I'm a good customer. My family appreciates the service he provides: knives, scissors, garden tools, and even a beaten-up push lawn mower work like new once he's finished with them.

The knife sharpener came from Italy years ago, speaks little English, and sometimes wears a tourist cap from Israel. He looks to be in his 80s, as does his competitor, also Italian-born. Their sharpening machines on wheels may be as old as they are. Both have been working this leafy central Toronto neighbourhood for years, but I know that one summer they won't return and that nobody will replace them. They did not come to Canada so that their children would be itinerant knife sharpeners.

An economist might say that the knife sharpener is a worker with "complementary skills" to those of the existing labour force;

because his profession is one that Canadian-born people do not follow, he provides a service that, had he not emigrated here, would not be available. By coming to their doors, he saves his customers time and money and gives them a reason to prolong the life of implements that might otherwise be thrown out.

Thousands of such immigrants contribute to the life of the downtown Toronto neighbourhood in which I live. The nearby retail strip on Bloor Street is a rich mixture of Korean and Hispanic, reflecting two recent waves of immigrants, with a few remnants of previous inflows of Hungarians and southern Europeans. Not all are successful, of course, as evidenced by the foreign-born panhandlers plying their trade. But most are hard-working shopkeepers and restaurant owners doing their best to achieve the better life they came to Canada to find.

This is not a book against immigration. I would never write such a book, because I am in favour of immigration. Were I not, I would not choose to live in one of the most diverse neigh-bourhoods in Canada and would not have sent my son to a local primary school that counted no fewer than 40 mother tongues among its students.

This is, however, a book critical of current immigration and refugee policies in Canada. One of the many absurdities that surround discussion of immigration in Canada is the assump-tion that anyone who questions current policy must be opposed to immigration. For those eager to preserve the status quo, informed discussion perhaps comes with risks. But if Canadians want an immigration program that benefits both newcomers and the existing population, that aids and shelters genuine refugees, and that is sustainable because it has public support, then the current system needs to be discussed, understood, and questioned. And – I will argue – overhauled.

Almost all countries have immigrants; relatively few have organized immigration programs that set out numerical targets and selection criteria. Among those few, Canada once led the way in formulating policies that were good for the newcomers and for the country. We were the first to adopt universality, meaning equal treatment of applicants regardless of skin colour. We invented the points system, whereby the skills of would-be immigrants could be matched to the needs of the country. And the humanitarian side of our program was held in such high esteem that in 1986 the United Nations awarded it the Nansen Medal for service to refugees. That was Canada's immigration program through much of the post–World War II period. The current system doesn't even resemble it.

I am not alone in viewing the current system as a shambles. Tom Kent, the respected civil servant who played a key role in the 1960s in ridding the selection process of racial bias, has written that, because of the program's current disarray, "Canada's reputation for competent government is badly tarnished." William Bauer, the distinguished Canadian diplomat, a recipient of the Raoul Wallenberg Humanitarian Award and an expert on refugee matters, calls the current Canadian refugee system "massive corruption of the noble concept of political asylum." Jack Manion, a former deputy minister of immigration who also held other senior federal posts, calls the status quo a "shocking and scandalous mess."

Some supporters of the current immigration program portray critics of the status quo as xenophobes, racists, and members of the extreme right. But Kent, Bauer, and Manion don't fit that stereotype. Neither do I.

Like most Canadians, I am a member of the radical middle. The radical middle is concerned with what works best, not with whether a particular program or policy fits some preconceived ideology. Show us that private companies can run roads better than government can and we say, Bring on the companies. Demonstrate that car insurance is a natural monopoly most efficiently operated by the state and we say, Boot out the companies and let government take over. That's why the radical middle is radical: it is ready to accept change. Ideologues of the left, by contrast, never want to see the role of government reduced, while those of the right reject public car insurance not because it doesn't work but because, for them, it is ideologically incorrect.

Public opinion polls consistently show that Canadians want the immigration program changed, not because they are xenophobes but because the immigration program doesn't work. Most support immigration but want more manageable numbers of immigrants and want abuse of the refugee system stopped. It is the minority of ideologues of both left and right who support the status quo. Both extremes support very high immigration levels, and neither cares whether the new immigrants are literate or have skills the Canadian economy needs.

Because there is so much confusion, and because critics of the status quo are routinely and falsely labelled "right-wing," it is important to understand how ideology creates odd couples. Two different facets of "left" and "right" are at play in the immigration debate: the economic and the cultural. The economic left supports policies that narrow the gap between rich and poor. As we shall see in chapter 5, immigration depresses wages, thereby transferring income from workers to employers. The economic left, therefore, should resist high immigration levels. For the same reason, the economic right should – and does – support them.

The cultural left, though, is at odds with the economic left. It wants more immigration because it loathes the culture of the Canadian majority, people of British, French, and other European origins. Most immigrants are non-white people of non-European origin. The cultural left looks forward to the day when non-Europeans are dominant. The cultural right, on the other hand, wants to preserve the cultural status quo. So the cultural right is at odds with the economic right, the cultural left with the economic left. And the cultural left finds itself in uneasy cohabitation with the economic right.

How does this work in practice? The economic left is moribund in Canada. The cultural left has seized control of Canada's only left-wing party, the New Democrats, and so there is no one to defend the interests of wage earners on the immigration issue. The economic right, on the other hand, makes its voice heard clearly. All major business organizations support an immigration policy that serves their interests, as do most business writers and ultra-conservative columnists.

Because the economic left is silent, most debate about immigration policy takes place within the political right. The cultural conservatives are quiet in Canada, a country ruled like no other by political correctness. But they dominate the immigration debate in Europe and are powerful in the United States as well. Patrick Buchanan, a cultural conservative, wrote a best-selling book, *The Death of the West*, arguing that the survival of American civilization is imperilled by, among other things, excessive non-white immigration. Meanwhile, the *Wall Street Journal*, the standard-bearer of economic conservatism, has for years campaigned for an end to all restrictions on immigration.

The positions of Buchanan and the *Wall Street Journal* are both extreme and thus of little interest to the vast majority of Canadians, who occupy the middle of the political spectrum. They want neither unrestricted immigration nor an end to it. They know the immigration system is broken and they want it fixed. But few understand the extent of the damage inflicted on it by Brian Mulroney and Jean Chrétien. The damage is three-fold: the number of immigrants admitted annually is too high; the proportion of skilled immigrants is too low; and the refugee determination system cannot distinguish between real refugees and fraudulent ones.

Annual intake, which used to fluctuate according to economic conditions, was raised under Mulroney to unprecedented levels and made permanent. In the earlier system, intake was adjusted according to the absorptive capacity of the economy and labour market conditions. The policy of permanent high immigration, instituted by Mulroney and carried on by Chrétien, is unique in the world. It puts needless stress on both the host society and the most recent newcomers themselves, whose entry to the Canadian economy is made more difficult by the need to compete with a relentless flow of new immigrants.

Canada accepts about a million immigrants every four years, twice as many per capita as the United States and almost twice as many per capita as Australia. The comparison with those nations is apt because they are the other two major immigration-receiving countries with organized programs. Moreover, they are the only countries that share Canada's demographic structure: the populations of all three are dominated by large cohorts of post-war baby boomers whose eldest members will begin entering retirement in the next decade. Both the United States and Australia want immigration, but, unlike Canada, neither sees any demographic need for massive amounts of it.

As for the composition of that inflow, the country that invented the points system now gives preference to unskilled immigrants; only about 23 percent of immigrants are even assessed for literacy and other skills. The rest are admitted either as relatives of a selected (independent) immigrant, as relatives of someone else already living in Canada, or as refugees.

A refugee is someone who is fleeing persecution and requires safe haven. Canadians are generous and eager to help real refugees. That generosity is abused, though, because Canada now admits, at great cost to taxpayers, thousands of people who are not refugees by the standards of the rest of the world while offering meagre support to the 21 million genuine refugees stranded in Third World camps.

The situation cries out for reasoned, informed discussion, yet little such discussion is heard. That's because, more than any other area of public policy, immigration is encrusted with empty rhetoric, emotionalism, false assumptions, and quaint notions that no longer make sense. The objective of this pro-immigration book is to pierce the fog of nonsense and deception by introducing some clear thinking about the subject.

As prime minister, Jean Chrétien paid little attention to criticism of his immigration policy. He was content to put weak ministers in the immigration and multiculturalism portfolios and to let the clients and beneficiaries of the program call the shots. Until September 11, 2001, that is. The destruction of that day marked the beginning of the end of the Liberals' immigration policy – not because Chrétien was ashamed of presiding over a "shocking and scandalous mess," but because the Americans told him to fix it. Our mismanagement of immigration, the U.S. government believed, was endangering the safety of U.S. citizens. If Canada wanted its goods to flow freely across the U.S. border, it had to make changes.

That doesn't mean Canada's program needs to be made identical to that of the Americans, whose system is far from perfect. What it does mean is that we need to rebuild our system in a manner that serves the collective interests of all Canadians; in so doing, we will restore the confidence of the Americans as well. Canada's immigration program, this book will argue, needs to be taken back from the special interests that have captured it and returned to the Canadian people.

CHAPTER ONE

THE END OF INNOCENCE

In June 1999, a dilapidated fishing boat left Fujian province on the Chinese coast and began chugging its way across the Pacific Ocean. For the 123 people on board it was the start of a miserable voyage in filthy conditions. Thirty-nine days later, on July 20, they caught their first glimpse of "Gold Mountain," the Chinese expression for North America, a promised land of boundless wealth. If they felt any joy, however, it was short-lived. The Canadian Coast Guard intercepted the rusting vessel off Nootka Sound, 300 kilometres north of Victoria, British Columbia.

The authorities took the arrivals, who had hoped to slip into Canada undetected, to Canadian Forces Base Esquimalt, near Victoria, and gave them food, clothing, and the first showers and clean beds they had had since leaving China. The generosity of the Canadian hosts did not end there. The migrants were given free access to lawyers, who informed them they were entitled to claim refugee status, which they soon did.

After they made their claims, they were released pending

hearings. Most then did as they had planned all along: made their way illegally to the United States, where, no doubt, they are now working in sweatshops, in restaurants, or as prostitutes to pay off their debts of US$40,000 or more to the smugglers, known as "snakeheads," who had arranged their transit across the Pacific.

A few months later, on December 14, 1999, a U.S. customs inspector in Port Angeles, Washington, stopped a car that had just disembarked from a ferry after the 35-kilometre crossing of the Strait of Juan de Fuca from Victoria. The driver, an Algerian named Ahmed Ressam, seemed nervous. He had good reason to be. The trunk of his rental car turned out to contain 60 kilograms of explosives and detonator components. His target, it turned out, had been Los Angeles International Airport – ironically, LAX in airline code. "Lax" was a word increasingly applied to the Canadian immigration system.

Ressam had been living in Canada for five years, even though French authorities had warned the Canadian government that he was a terrorist and even though he had not bothered to show up for his refugee hearing. Instead of deporting him, the Canadians had let him live freely, provided him with welfare, and issued him a Canadian passport (in a false name). They had even allowed him to re-enter the country after he'd travelled to Afghanistan to train with Osama bin Laden's al-Qaeda terrorist organization.

These two incidents tarnished the already discredited image of the Canadian immigration and refugee system. Two years after the capture of Ressam, a senior official in the immigration department was still practically in shock over the events of 1999. "We had been so naive in thinking that everything in the immigration program was positive," he recalled. "We thought there couldn't be a negative."

That first migrant ship intercepted off the B.C. coast had been followed, in ensuing months, by three more ships also found, when intercepted, to be full of Chinese nationals. "It wasn't like these people were coming to an airport, where they see an immigration officer and make a refugee claim. These are people who don't even want to be here or be detected. I remember my dentist asking me, 'Why would we be so hospitable to them?' I didn't have a good answer. Why would we give them due process? Feed them and care about them? Canada had assumed that people who came here wanted to become Canadian citizens. All of a sudden that wasn't the case. It seemed like all generosity for no gain.

"And then Ressam gets caught with explosives. What do you mean, people would come here with false documents and plot to kill people? How could they do that?" To critics of Canada's immigration program, neither event was particularly surprising, but this official was genuinely shaken. "It was," he said, "the end of innocence."

Or was it? Neither the minister of immigration at the time, Elinor Caplan, nor the prime minister, Jean Chrétien, seemed unduly alarmed. Despite the uproar caused by the Ressam case, Canada blithely continued to operate a refugee system in which terrorists could arrive without identification and, simply by claiming to be fleeing persecution, gain release into Canadian society to do as they pleased.

It was not the first time the Canadian government, head in the sand, had refused to acknowledge the obvious links between its immigration program and terrorism. Back in 1985, 329 people, most of them Canadian citizens, had been murdered when a bomb exploded aboard an Air India jet en route from Montreal to London, New Delhi, and Bombay. The attack, the most devastating act of aviation terrorism to that date, was believed to have been carried out by Sikh extremists who had immigrated to Canada.

The real end of innocence came on September 11, 2001. The terrorists who struck the World Trade Center and the Pentagon had not entered the United States from Canada, but this detail was hardly reassuring. The Canadian Security Intelligence Service (CSIS) had acknowledged in May 2000 that Islamic terrorists were operating in Canada. The 19 hijackers of September 11 may not have used Canada as a base, but Ressam and two accomplices, Bouabide Chamchi and Abdel Hakim Tizegha, *had* entered the United States from Canada. So had Nabil al-Marabh, identified in 1999 by U.S. intelligence as an al-Qaeda operative. So had Gazi Ibrahim Abu Mezer, whose plan to blow up a Brooklyn subway station was thwarted by a tip to police from his roommate. In any case, the salient fact for Canadians was not that Islamist fanatics could and did enter the United States from Canada but that the followers of bin Laden had identified all Western "infidels," not just Americans, as the objects of their hatred.

Islamists, unlike peaceful adherents of Islam, wish to destroy secular governments everywhere and replace them with theocratic dictatorships. Because of the spread of fanatical Islamism, Canada now has deadly enemies within its own borders; indisputably, immigration has become a matter of national security. Other terrorist organizations – the Irish Republican Army, for example, and the Tamil Tigers – have long been active in Canada, but their targets are far from our shores. The government has never been overly concerned about having people in our midst associated with terrorist organizations that kill innocent civilians thousands of kilometres away or that murder foreign-born Canadian citizens travelling on foreign airplanes. But Islamists want to kill Canadians *in* Canada: Ressam said as much when he testified during his trial in the United States, that he and an associate, Samir Ait Mohamed, had plotted to detonate a bomb in Montreal.

After September 11, the Canadian government's struggle to deal with the new complexities of global terrorism was painful to watch. National security is a collective interest that overrides special interests, yet the Liberal government seemed unable to grasp that the collective well-being of all Canadians, rather than the demands of the clients and beneficiaries of the immigration program, must take priority.

No federal program has a more profound effect on Canada and its future than immigration. Because Canada is the biggest accepter of immigrants in the world, admitting twice as many people relative to existing population as any other country, the policies we adopt will profoundly influence the size of the Canadian population and of our major cities. Immigration policies affect our environment. And because immigration enriches some at the expense of others, it has a major, if little-known, impact on the way income is distributed among Canadians.

Immigration to Canada is part of a global phenomenon of incalculable consequence. Hundreds of millions of people wish to get from poor countries to rich ones, and growing numbers achieve this goal illegally; the United States alone is home to an estimated 8 million illegal immigrants. The question of how to moderate and control the unprecedented global mass movement of people is one of the thorniest issues affecting the world's governments.

Canada is part of the problem, rather than part of the solution. As other countries have pointed out, our wide-open refugee system encourages would-be economic migrants to leave their homes and come here whether or not they qualify for admission. They come because Canada's Immigration and Refugee Board (IRB) allows them to circumvent the regular immigration program by awarding Geneva Convention refugee status to thousands of people who have no chance of obtaining it elsewhere. Refugee status is a precious commodity: with it comes entitlement to welfare, medicare, and other social programs, as well as eventual acceptance as a landed immigrant, which in turn carries with it the right to sponsor relatives to come to Canada.

Migration experts call this the "pull factor": the IRB's world-beating acceptance rate for refugee claims pulls people out of their homes in the Third World and delivers them, among other places, into the hands of smugglers. By maintaining the current refugee system, Canada unwittingly stimulates the international people-smuggling business, a multi-billion-dollar criminal enterprise that may be as lucrative as the global trade in illegal drugs.

The malfunctioning of the IRB is not news. Its chief flaw is obvious: it is staffed by amateurs, including patronage appointees and members of organizations that advocate on behalf of refugee claimants. An independent study of immigration policy in 1997 made the sound proposal that the IRB's amateurs be replaced by professional public servants staffing a new Protection Agency responsible both for adjudicating claims made in Canada and for selecting refugees overseas.

The government paid no more attention to this proposal than it had to others for fixing various broken pieces of the immigration program. For example, many sponsors of family members renege on their commitments to ensure that their relatives do not wind up on welfare. Several years ago, Don DeVoretz, an immigration expert at Simon Fraser University, suggested an obvious solution: sponsors should be required to post bond. He was ignored. Why? For the same reasons that the Chrétien government resists suggestions that a higher percentage of immigrants be screened for skills, or that every undocumented, unidentified refugee claimant be detained in the interests of public safety: the norm in other countries.

Implicit in such ideas for change is the assumption that the immigration program should serve the best interests of the country. For the Liberal government, however, the point is not how immigration can best serve the country but how it can best serve the Liberals. Why would it replace the IRB merely because the IRB cannot distinguish real refugees from phony ones? The IRB is a wonderful vehicle with which to reward faithful party members with highly paid jobs. As for pursuing defaulting sponsors, that might displease the organizations that claim to represent immigrants. These organizations have the power to deliver votes; acting in accordance with their wishes enhances the Liberal Party's long-term prospects for staying in power.

Nor does it matter that polls show widespread dissatisfaction with immigration policy; the politicians know that few Canadians base their voting decisions on immigration issues. Immigration did became an important issue in Australia's federal election in 2001, and perhaps it will be decisive in some future Canadian election. But it hasn't happened yet. And until it does, tailoring the program to the desires of its clients and beneficiaries – rather than to the best interests of the Canadian population – is a winning political strategy.

The Liberals have long understood that they could do whatever they liked with immigration and its spinoff, multiculturalism. This attitude, at its worst, descends into outright contempt for the Canadian people. On March 22, 2001, Hedy Fry, then secretary of state for multiculturalism, stated in the House of Commons that crosses were burning on lawns in Prince George, British Columbia, "as we speak." As it turned out, no crosses were burning in Prince George as Fry spoke, nor had any burned when she wasn't speaking. Her statement was a fabrication that slandered the people of Prince George by comparing them to the lynch mobs of the Ku Klux Klan. She later offered an apology but no explanation of why she had made the bizarre allegation. That Fry was not fired from cabinet immediately after this ludicrous performance (rather than 10 months later) was proof that her portfolio was not seen as important.

Multiculturalism – as people in places such as the former Yugoslavia know only too well – is a serious matter. One of our many immigration myths is that people of many backgrounds live harmoniously in Canada because we have multiculturalism as official policy. In fact, Canadians of various cultural backgrounds coexist harmoniously not because Canada is multicultural but because it isn't.

Canada's urban population is one of the most diverse in the world, true; but diversity and multiculturalism are very different things. Diversity refers to superficial differences, such as skin colour or dress. Such differences are accepted by most Canadians, and embraced enthusiastically by many, as adding interest and vitality to the urban landscape. But culture goes deeper, and cultural practices profoundly different from those of the majority culture – polygamy, for example – are not tolerated in Canada. Overt attempts by minorities to maintain elements of their culture that conflict with deeply held beliefs of the majority have been rare; but when such conflicts have arisen – when, for example, a Sikh member of the RCMP sought the right to wear a turban – the "multicultural" harmony of which Canadians are so proud has proven to be paper-thin. Canadian multiculturalism, in short, takes for granted an edited version of the minority cultures.

Well before the world woke up to the reality of radical Islamism, there were signs that not all Canada's minorities were willing to censor their beliefs to conform to those of the majority. In February 1989, Iran's ruler, the Ayatollah Khomeini, issued a fatwa, an edict, sentencing to death the British novelist Salman Rushdie and all others involved in the publication of Rushdie's novel *The Satanic Verses* because of the satirical treatment of Islam in the book. Canadians, who take for granted freedom of expression, waited for Canadian Muslim leaders to denounce Khomeini's outrageous incitement to murder. More than a decade later, they are still waiting.

In 1995 the political columnist Richard Gwyn wrote that "one test exists to determine when we'll start to become a multicultural country. This would be when the Muslim Canadian community breaks its silence of now six years to denounce the *fatwa* death sentence against [Rushdie]." Actually, by neither endorsing nor denouncing the fatwa, the Canadian Muslims were practising a sort of passive multiculturalism. Denouncing the fatwa would have been an act not of multiculturalism but of assimilation, of embracing mainstream Canadian values, a step Muslims were not prepared to take.

Canada is a secular country in which religion is a private matter and the right to offend adherents of religious (or any other) orthodoxy is protected by law. But many Canadian Muslims come from countries where Islam has the force of law and freedom of expression is non-existent. They may not have agreed with the ayatollah's edict, but neither did they accept Rushdie's freedom to express himself as he wished.

This fundamental clash of values illustrates how poorly defined and misunderstood was the Canadian government's concept of official multiculturalism. "If Canada is really a multicultural country," an orthodox Muslim might well have asked, "why should I feel embarrassed about cheering the ayatollah? Why, if Rushdie comes here, can't I kill him? That's what my culture demands, and Canada is supposed to be multicultural."

The answer is that the politicians have misled us: Canada is diverse but not multicultural. The crucial difference is that multiculturalism is divisive and diversity is not. Multiculturalism is divisive because different cultures have irreconcilable values. Diversity is not divisive because Canada is built not around an ethnicity or a religion but rather around a shared belief in the values of democracy and individual freedom. But if a belief in democracy unites us, and freedom of speech is essential to democracy, what happens when a powerful minority group refuses to accept that basic value? Doesn't that refusal threaten the cohesion of Canadian society?

In its innocence, the Canadian government saw no ominous portents in the Rushdie affair, despite the Muslim community's distaste for democratic values. The government clung to its fuzzy policy of multiculturalism without ever spelling out its limits. In the meantime, criticism mounted. Besides Gwyn, many other prominent journalists and authors – Neil Bissoondath, Bharati Mukherjee, Laura Sabia, and Robert Fulford among them – wondered why a government would encourage permanent ethnic divisions among its citizenry. "Official multiculturalism, the automatic classification of citizens according to race and ancestry, was a bad idea in the beginning," Fulford wrote in the *Globe and Mail*, "and in time will probably be seen as one of the gigantic mistakes of recent public policy in Canada."

Not long after September 11, the political philosopher Michael Ignatieff suggested that the time had come to lay down explicit rules about multiculturalism. How, Ignatieff wondered, could we continue to tolerate the propensity of some Canadians to lend support to terrorism in other countries? The fact was that terror is a well-established Canadian export. Immigrants from Ireland, Croatia, Sri Lanka, and many other places have for years financed terrorist organizations in the lands they left behind. "The disturbing possibility," Ignatieff wrote, "is that Canada is not an asylum from hatred but an incubator of hatred." Hatred cannot be outlawed, but support for terrorizing and murdering civilians can and should be. Canada must, Ignatieff concluded, "have laws for the prosecution of anyone in Canada who aids, abets, encourages or incites acts of terror."

Until September 11, the Liberal government had not been prepared to pass such a law. In December 1999, it had signed the International Convention for the Suppression of the Financing of Terrorism but, almost two years later, when the terrorists struck the World Trade Center and the Pentagon, no Canadian law prohibited terrorist fundraising.

Why the inertia? Because the good of the country and the world conflicted with the demands of Liberal supporters in the ethnic communities. The international convention that Canada signed called for the criminalization of the collection of funds to support terrorism. Yet by September 11, 2001, all the Liberals had done was introduce a bill stripping charitable status from organizations that raised money for terrorists. Organizations would still legally be able to raise money to terrorize and murder innocent civilians abroad, but their donors wouldn't get tax deductions. Even this modest measure was stalled because of the storm of criticism it provoked. Typical was the reaction of the Islamic Supreme Council of Canada, which said the legislation would "smear the reputation of humanitarian organizations."

Despite the Air India bombing, despite Ahmed Ressam, despite the unambiguous assertion of CSIS officials that 50 terrorist organizations were operating in Canada, innocence reigned in Ottawa. How else to explain the decision of Paul Martin, then finance minister, and Maria Minna, then minister of international cooperation, to attend a fundraising dinner in Toronto sponsored by the Federation of Associations of Canadian Tamils (FACT).

The dinner, in May 2000, was meant to honour the Tamil new year. According to a Sri Lankan news report, those attending the dinner "were amused to see Canadian ministers and politicians walking around wishing 'Happy New Year' to everybody" – amused because the new year had actually begun a month earlier. But the dinner was embarrassing in a deeper way. Before it was held, Canada's high commission in Sri Lanka had warned Martin not to attend because FACT is a front for one of the most vicious terrorist organizations in the world, the Liberation Tigers of Tamil Eelam (LTTE), the Tamil Tigers. The high commission's advice was based on information from CSIS and the U.S. State Department.

What could have shown more forcefully the subservience of the Liberal government to organized ethnic groups than the attendance of a senior cabinet member at a dinner whose sponsors were linked to the organization that had invented suicide bombing and had caused 60,000 deaths? Martin's behaviour was even more appalling than Fry's because it was deliberate. Whereas Fry had blurted out something she must instantly have recognized as indefensible, and regretted, Martin had plenty of time to consider the warnings of his diplomatic and intelligence officials. Not only did he ignore the warnings, he had the audacity to label those who questioned his attendance at the dinner "un-Canadian." And he seemed to give no thought to how demoralizing his behaviour must have been to the members of the Canadian Tamil community who have suffered retribution for daring to oppose the Tigers.

The affair was front-page news in Sri Lanka. It caused a diplomatic row. Martin's attendance was a disservice to his country but, so he must have thought, a service to his party. In the Liberals' pre–September 11 innocence, immigration and multiculturalism were about service to the party, about securing and solidifying loyal, long-term political support. That's why the Chrétien government thought it was enough merely to sign an international convention against terrorist fundraising; it wasn't necessary to actually do anything that might be politically inconvenient.

Similarly, it was enough for the government to announce its intention to eventually replace the IMM 1000, the paper document Canada issues to identify a landed immigrant. There was no urgency; it didn't seem to matter to the Chrétien cabinet that the IMM 1000 was easily duplicated and that terrorists and other foreign criminals could use it to get driver's licences and social insurance numbers, creating an apparently legitimate identity. No need for action.

Within hours of the destruction of the World Trade Center, fingers were pointed. Canada was partly to blame, some Americans claimed, because the terrorists must have taken advantage of Canada's lax immigration and refugee system. In fact, the terrorists had taken advantage of laxity in the U.S. system, but Canadians who pointed defensively to this fact were disingenuous in suggesting the Canadian system was sound. The terrorists might just as easily have used Canada as their base.

The Chrétien government had to admit, belatedly, that immigration is indeed a matter of national security. Suddenly the world's longest undefended border was of pressing concern. Far fewer illegal immigrants enter the United States across the northern border than across a southern border half as long, but September 11 reminded the world that a handful of people bent on destruction can do horrific damage. The Americans knew that Ressam had been carrying a valid Canadian passport, and that he was not a fluke but rather a symptom of flaws in the way Canada deals with dangerous "aliens" (the official U.S. term for foreigners). And they were newly awake to the dangers inherent in having a porous border so close to their economic and political hearts: New York City and Washington, D.C.

The Canadian government might have considered American fears exaggerated, but it couldn't dismiss them. Canada, after all, lives off its exports, and the United States buys 85 percent of them. After the attacks, the Americans imposed strict controls on incoming traffic from Canada, causing lengthy delays at the border and severely disrupting trade.

The restrictions were a message to the Chrétien government. The message was received. The border had to be kept open, and that meant satisfying the government of President George W. Bush that the Canada-U.S. border did not represent a deadly threat. Paul Martin announced $1.2 billion for border infrastructure and security. In the meantime, Washington had dispatched the National Guard to supplement its border patrol.

Two new words appeared in the lexicon of U.S.-Canada relations: "harmonization" and "perimeter." These ideas were closely linked. If the two countries' immigration and refugee policies were harmonized, a security perimeter could be established around all of Canada and the United States, thereby eliminating checkpoints along the border and facilitating trade. "We want to move the border out from between Maine and Canada to [between] North America and the rest of the world," explained Maine governor Angus King.

The Canadian government wasn't ready to go that far, although the Canadian people were: an Ipsos-Reid poll released in October 2001 found more than 80 percent in favour of a joint North American security perimeter and a harmonized immigration and refugee system. These poll results seemed not to impress the government. The Liberals benefit from running the world's largest, loosest immigration and refugee program, and while they understood that American fears had to be addressed, they seemed unable to grasp that the world had changed.

Elinor Caplan claimed that an immigration bill, C-11, that had been working its way through Parliament in the preceding months would address security concerns. The new law, which came into force in June 2002, did nothing of the sort; its main impact, explained James Bissett, a former head of the immigration service, would be to make it easier for terrorists and war criminals to use endless legal appeals to stay in Canada.

In the aftermath of September 11, however, the government was forced to take some small steps to satisfy the Americans. John Manley, the foreign affairs minister at the time, was named head of a new cabinet committee on public security. The government ordered security tightened at airports; it promised to buy the latest fingerprint scanners and bomb detection equipment. Caplan announced that the easily forged IMM 1000 landed immigrant document would be replaced by a high-tech card. And in December 2001, the Liberals passed the Anti-Terrorism Act, making fundraising for organizations supporting terrorism a crime. The law provided for the creation of a list of such organizations, banned the harbouring of terrorists, and gave the police new rights to investigate suspected terrorists.

A debate ensued in the media over whether this legislation was an unnecessary infringement of civil liberties. Unmentioned amid these philosophical arguments was the simple fact that the government had failed to address the real security issues: our elevated immigration levels and our malfunctioning refugee system.

David Harris, former chief of strategic planning for the Canadian Security Intelligence Service, runs a consulting firm specializing in national security and counterterrorism. In Ottawa, a few weeks after September 11, 2001, he was in shock over the government's blindness to the dangers inherent in the way it manages immigration. The failure to correct the program's fundamental flaws, he said, is "grand-scale avoidance of the issues. It reminds me of a cartoon I saw of someone talking to someone else in a normal way when the other person has an elephant on his shoulder."

There's good reason why no other country has, or even contemplates, immigration on the fantastic scale that Canada has. It's dangerous. It's impossible to do all but the most cursory checks on an annual intake of 250,000 people. "Even if you've got the most stupendously competent security systems," Harris said, "there's no way you can give any kind of assurance about these people. That number is a deadly threat." Canada has no reason to assume that immigrants who arrive legally are correctly identified. "We're dealing with a world that is so unstable. And a majority of people are coming from unstable regions where record-keeping, if it exists, is notoriously unreliable."

Then there is the refugee system. After September 11, Caplan had boasted that "our laws are amongst the toughest in the world when it comes to inadmissibility for criminality and terrorism." This statement was as untruthful as Hedy Fry's claim that crosses were burning on the lawns of Prince George. Canada's asylum system is an invitation to terrorists and criminals because Canada neither excludes nor detains undocumented arrivals. Unless a refugee claimant admits to being a criminal or terrorist, or otherwise arouses suspicion, the unidentified claimant is free to disappear into Canada or find his way across the U.S. border.

Refugee claimants are not detained even if the IRB rules them inadmissible. The government naively trusts that they will turn themselves in later, to be deported; of course, many are never seen again. For such reasons Canada's refugee system, said Harris, "is pretty close to self-destructively insane."

If the solutions look simple, they are – on the face of it. The annual intake could be brought down to the same per capita number as those of the United States and Australia, which is the level Canada had before the Mulroney government raised immigration to new heights. The IRB could be replaced with a body that applies the Geneva Convention the way the rest of the Western world does. And Canada, like other industrialized countries, could stop admitting refugee claimants who arrive not from the homeland they're fleeing but from another safe country where they could have claimed asylum.

But the Chrétien government, said Harris, has no wish to reform immigration in the interests of national security. It would rather "trade off our civil liberties in order to empower immigration racketeers." Racketeers? "The politicians who feed off immigration for votes and political careers," said Harris. "People at senior government level who have every-thing in the short term to gain from continuing this racket and much to lose from not doing so."

Recently the government has taken some small steps. The removal of Elinor Caplan from the immigration portfolio in the cabinet shuffle of January 2002 was perhaps part of that process. She was, commented a *Globe and Mail* editorial, "an 'open door' kind of liberal who appeared philosophically uncomfortable with the law-and-order toughness Canadians were seeking after September 11."

This seems unfair to Caplan. True, her post–September 11 performance had been erratic, but there was no evidence that Chrétien had given her a mandate to make national security a priority. Chrétien was not a strong and inspiring leader in the mould of British prime minister Tony Blair. He seemed to see himself less as a leader than as a headwaiter whose job was to ensure that all the loyal customers in the Liberal restaurant got what they had ordered.

The Chrétien government prefers to respond rather than to lead, and Chrétien has made an art of not angering Liberal supporters. Many ethnic communities vote en masse for the Liberals; their support is pivotal in more than 30 ridings. Perhaps it was inevitable that his government would use its immigration program to serve the needs of its clients. Caplan's mandate had been to please her "stakeholders," the ethnic communities and organizations and lawyers and non-governmental agencies attached to the immigration program. Pleasing them meant maintaining a large flow of immigrants and refugees with as few impediments to entry as possible.

A respectable veneer had to be put on this partisan program to minimize public hostility to it. Thus Caplan made the standard claims that immigration brings great economic benefits to Canada and that a high intake of newcomers is essential to ensure that, given our aging population, we don't run out of live bodies to keep the place functioning. All reputable research, including that commissioned by the government itself, refutes these ideas, which made endorsing them in public an embarrassing and thankless task. Caplan seemed to have performed it as well as could be expected.

Her problem, like that of her successor, Denis Coderre, was that the government had no credible rationale for its immigration program. It wasn't for lack of excellent research; the research existed, but the government knew that it didn't fit the policy. In 1991 the former Economic Council of Canada had produced a thorough study of the economic impacts of immigration, and under Mulroney the Department of Health and Welfare had commissioned a far-reaching analysis of Canada's demographic needs. More recently, Don DeVoretz at Simon Fraser and other scholars had described the declining economic performance of immigrants because of the rising proportion of unskilled people among them. And Roderic Beaujot of the

University of Western Ontario, Canada's leading expert on the relationship between demographics and immigration, had produced an analysis of the best Canadian studies.

The research was not acted on because immigration was never viewed from the perspective of national interest. September 11 taught everyone that immigration is indeed a national security issue. And national security – the protection of the population from harm – is the first duty of any government. The time has come to base immigration on national interest. First, we must ask ourselves some fundamental questions.

Who gets in? That's the most fundamental question. It's the question immigration policy must answer. Deciding who gets into Canada and who doesn't means deciding what we want immigration to do for the country. It means determining why we have immigration in the first place. It means ascertaining where the national interest lies.

Advocates of the status quo often try to shut off debate by labelling critics "racists." To those who live off the current immigration system, "racist" does not mean what *The Oxford English Dictionary* says it means: someone who believes in "the theory that distinctive human characteristics and abilities are determined by race." Instead, this highly charged word has been retooled to mean "disadvantageous to those who profit from the immigration program."

A government-appointed commission in 1997 proposed that a requirement for admission to Canada should be the ability to speak one of our two official languages. This was denounced by the immigration industry as "racist," though it was obviously not racist by the dictionary definition. Millions of Asians and blacks from dozens of countries, including Jamaica, Vietnam, Hong Kong, Haiti, and Nigeria, speak English or French; millions of whites from places like Russia, Romania, Portugal, and Poland don't. The word made sense only in its uniquely Canadian application. Thousands of jobs and many millions of dollars in government grants to immigrant-serving agencies depend on a steady supply of non-English-speakers for English as a second language (ESL) programs. These programs and jobs would disappear if arriving immigrants spoke English.

If the misuse of language were not enough of an impediment to rational discussion of immigration policy, the presence of hidden agendas is another. Perhaps it is because immigration is such a sensitive topic that many people are reluctant to say what they really mean.

My own agenda is open. I believe that the immigration program belongs to the people of Canada, not to any political party or special interest groups. I believe Canada should admit newcomers without regard to the colour of their skin. I believe we should give preference to skilled immigrants because they are the ones an advanced economy most needs and therefore the ones most likely to succeed. And I believe the humanitarian aspect of the program should be designed to help those most in need.

To help readers decipher what they may read or hear about immigration elsewhere, here are the four major groups with hidden agendas.

The cultural conservatives: These people want immigration stopped, or sharply curtailed, because they do not want to see the dominant culture of Canada, that of the descendants of the original European settlers, challenged by non-white people of non-European cultures.

The cultural radicals: These are the people who think books by "dead white males" should be removed from university courses. They look forward to the day when people of European ancestry are a minority in Canada. Rather than say so explicitly, they make outlandish claims for the alleged necessity of maintaining – or even raising – Canada's unrivalled immigration levels.

The financial stakeholders: A statement such as "I'm a land developer, so I want more immigration to drive up real estate prices" is unlikely to win public favour. Instead, the stakeholder will say, "Our population isn't replacing itself, so we need more immigration than we now have so there will be enough workers to support the baby boomers when they retire." This statement is nonsense, as we shall see in chapter 5, but if it is repeated often enough, and if enough gullible reporters can be found to publish it, people start to believe it.

The emotional stakeholders: Immigration is an emotional subject, so it is understandable that people form opinions based on emotion rather than reason. If Canada hadn't admitted our ancestors as immigrants, we ourselves wouldn't be here. Our ancestors may have had little education or been unable to speak English when they came, so why should we insist on such qualifications for today's immigrants? The short answer is that the Canada of 1902 had many opportunities for unskilled immigrants while the Canada of 2002 has mainly dead-end jobs, at or below minimum wage. The emotional supporters of the current immigration program don't want to hear such answers.

This emotionalism is built into official policy. One of the goals of Canada's immigration policy, for example, is family reunification. The concept derives from World War II and gets its emotional impact from that time when many husbands and wives in wartorn countries were separated from one another and sometimes from their children. Who would not help reunite such families?

In the parlance of Canadian immigration policy, however, "family reunification" has come to mean reuniting not immediate families that have been separated involuntarily but extended families that have separated voluntarily. It's not the social norm in Canada for extended families to live together; in fact, Canadian extended families are often spread out across the country. Why Canada should assume a moral obligation to reunite extended families from other countries whose members have separated of their own free will has never been explained.

This is not to say that liberal family reunification should not be part of immigration policy – if Canadians, having assessed the benefits and costs, decide that's what they want. Family reunification is beneficial to people who come because most of them, in so doing, are able to upgrade their standard of living. Sponsors already in Canada benefit emotionally from being reunited with relatives. They may benefit economically as well: for example, from the availability of babysitting or from the pooling of resources to buy a house.

These benefits, however, come at a cost to Canadian society. The expansion of family-class immigration over the past 20 years is the main reason the economic performance of immigrants has declined. Family-class immigrants need meet no criteria of skills or education; they can come even if they are illiterate in their own language. And so recent immigrants earn less, pay less tax, have higher unemployment rates, and make more use of welfare than previous cohorts of immigrants.

Increasing the supply of anything reduces its price. Immigration policy, with its emphasis on family reunification, increases the supply of unskilled labour. Unskilled workers were already ill paid before the Mulroney-Chrétien immigration policy made matters worse for them. Is it in the national interest to make our poorest citizens poorer? Is this one of the things we want our immigration program to achieve? It's certainly one of the things we need to discuss in formulating immigration policy.

Proponents of the current policy could argue that lower wages benefit not only employers but also consumers, who pay lower prices for the goods and services produced by low-paid workers. By depressing the cost of labour, immigrants help keep Canada's inflation rate low. These might be good reasons for continuing a liberal family reunification scheme despite its high social cost. But workers impoverished by this policy should also have a chance to offer opinions, based on a frank disclosure of costs and benefits.

Such disclosure has never been made. In Canada, it's considered rude even to mention the costs of immigration. George

Orwell pointed out that "at any given moment there is an orthodoxy, a body of ideas which it is assumed that all right thinking people will accept without question. It is not exactly forbidden to say this, that or the other, but it is 'not done' to say it, just as in mid-Victorian times it was 'not done' to mention trousers in the presence of a lady."

That describes precisely the debate over immigration in Canada. The "right-thinking" version is that immigration is good and more immigration is better. Immigration brings only benefits. To suggest that there might be negative consequences is in the worst taste; it's "not done."

In 1996 Don DeVoretz (who favours a generous intake of skilled immigrants) described in the *Vancouver Sun* the results of some technical research he and a colleague had published in a scholarly journal. They'd discovered that "workers in 47 major industries are losing jobs or suffering wage compression from immigration." This was stunning news; it could have transformed the way Canadians view immigration policy. It ought to have been on the front page of every newspaper. Instead, it was buried near the end of an opinion piece in a single newspaper. DeVoretz had mentioned trousers in front of a Victorian lady. Such faux pas, the media seem to have decided, are best ignored.

Meanwhile, when David Baxter, an economist allied with the real estate industry – a major beneficiary of high immigration levels – claimed that Canada needed a gigantic increase in immigration to compensate for our low fertility rate, the *Toronto Star* announced the "news," absurd as it was, in a page one banner headline.

Because of a lazy and compliant press, there is widespread ignorance about immigration and its impact on the country. In December 2001, Caplan, in one of her last acts as immigration minister, announced changes to the points system designed to attract those most likely to be successful and to arrest the declining economic performance of immigrants selected by the government for their skills. Here was a rare occasion: the government putting the interests of Canada ahead of those of the immigration lawyers, some of whose clients would be ineligible under the new rules.

Naturally, the lawyers erupted. So did members of Parliament from so-called ethnic ridings. Business columnists in the *National Post* and *Toronto Star*, like trained seals, reacted on cue, declaring that uneducated immigrants had succeeded in the past and should not be shut out in future. The columnists seemed to believe the new rules would apply to the majority of new immigrants.

Independent immigrants (sometimes called "skilled" or "economic" immigrants) are those selected by the government on the basis of their education and skills, both linguistic and occupational. The other two classes of immigrants are the family class, who get in because they are related to someone already living in Canada, and refugees. Less than a quarter of Canada's immigration intake is selected on the basis of skills and education. The government pretends otherwise by including accompanying immediate family members in the independent category, bringing the official total of skilled immigrants to 60 percent. This figure is misleading, though, for it includes a preponderance of spouses and small children, few of whom can claim to be skilled. More than three-quarters of immigrants, in short, need meet no educational criteria at all. So the angry columnists have little to fear: plenty of uneducated, unskilled newcomers will continue to arrive, regardless of changes to the points system.

The same columnists who misinterpreted Caplan's attempt to improve the points system claim that great economic benefits derive from immigration. There is no evidence to support that claim. By reducing the cost of labour, immigration makes possible the production of goods and services at lower cost, thereby delivering what the economist George Borjas calls an "immigration surplus" that benefits society as a whole. But this surplus is minimal, too small to serve as the economic justification for running a huge immigration program.

Countries with lots of immigrants do not outperform countries with few. There's no relationship between population growth, whether from natural increase or from immigration, and economic growth; the former does not imply the latter. If it did, citizens of China and India would be millionaires while those of European countries with relatively stable populations would have starved long ago.

As for Canada's demographic needs, they are no greater than those of most other industrialized countries, all of which have much less immigration than Canada has. Roderic Beaujot, the University of Western Ontario demographer, cautioned in a study published by the federal government: "We should not say that Canada 'needs' immigration either from a demographic or economic point of view."

Beaujot's statement, based on the best available research, contradicts the Liberal government and other supporters of current policy. Its implications are profound. They are that Canadians welcome immigrants not because we need them but because we want them. But if we don't need them, there's no reason to accept negative consequences from immigration. And the current program, in its disarray, is full of negative consequences.

Of course, immigration brings benefits. Our cities are cosmopolitan because of it, rich and dynamic. Some of Canada's most talented scientists, scholars, and entrepreneurs are immigrants. The likes of Michael Ondaatje, Rohinton Mistry, and Anita Rau Badami have helped make Canadian literature an extraordinary chorus that sings to the world. Innumerable foreign-born Canadians in every walk of life – cab drivers, chefs, doctors, plumbers, artists – make important contributions. That these people have been able to improve their lives and those of their families by choosing to live in Canada is not the least of the benefits immigration offers.

But if Canada does not need immigration, why accept negative consequences? Why accept a program that endangers the safety of the Canadian people? Innocence is dangerous; we cannot afford it. At the very least, the benefits of immigration should outweigh the costs. They no longer do. That is why Canada's immigration program desperately needs to be overhauled.

CHAPTER TWO

PEOPLE ON THE MOVE

DAVE LU WAS BORN IN 1971 IN LIU ZHAI, A FARMING village 1,600 kilometres from Beijing. He was the youngest of six children of illiterate peasants. He studied hard and was accepted at the best high school in Pei Xian county. The high school was in another village, so he said goodbye to his parents, brothers, and sisters and left the three-room family home for the first time. After high school he moved to Beijing to attend university.

In June 2001, he departed on a much longer journey. He boarded an Air Canada flight for Vancouver. In December of that year, Lu found himself living in a basement suite on the east side of the city, with his wife and infant son, and commuting an hour to an office building in the North Shore suburb of West Vancouver, where he worked for a lumber firm. He was struggling to attain functional English, struggling to figure out how this puzzling society works.

He keeps in touch with his parents, although they don't have a telephone. A neighbour has one, and once a month Lu calls the neighbour, who brings his parents to the phone. Lu, with glasses and close-cropped hair, is a serious and intent young man. Uprooting oneself from one's home is always difficult, and it's usually the most ambitious who attempt it. It would have been easier to stay in China, he said over Chinese food at a restaurant overlooking the waterfront, but China couldn't satisfy his ambitions. "I wanted to go out and see the world."

People have been wanting to go out and see the world since human beings first learned to walk. Perhaps Kennewick Man, leaving home for the first time, told his parents, "I want to go out and see the world."

The discovery of Kennewick Man on the banks of the Columbia River in Washington State reminded us how little we really know about how, and by whom, North America was first populated. On July 28, 1996, two college students watching a boat race found a skull and, assuming it belonged to a murder victim, called the police, who called the local coroner. The coroner called a forensic anthropologist, whose services he used when he needed to distinguish between recent murder victims and old bodies. The two of them went out to the river and found most of the dead man's bones.

They assembled the skeleton and decided they were dealing with a "Caucasoid" male, between 40 and 55 years old and about five feet nine inches tall – much taller than the prehistoric natives who had been discovered in that part of the Pacific Northwest. These remains, they were certain, weren't those of a native Indian. Probably, they reasoned, the bones were those of one of the early pioneers or trappers who had settled Washington State in the 19th century.

There turned out to be problems with that theory. For one, a spear point embedded in the thigh bone was widely used as long as 9,000 years ago. For another, when they sent one of the bones to California for radiocarbon dating, they learned that the skeleton was between 9,300 and 9,600 years old.

This was astonishing. Conventional theory had it that

North America was peopled by three waves of Asian migrants, the first coming about 12,000 years ago, when humans were able to cross a land bridge from Siberia to Alaska. These migrants were the ancestors of the native people who live today in North and South America. But Kennewick Man doesn't resemble an Asian or a native American. In fact, the cast made of his skull reveals him to be a dead ringer for Captain Jean-Luc Picard, the *Star Trek* character played by Patrick Stewart, a native of Mirfield, England.

What was somebody who looked like an Englishman doing in the Pacific Northwest 9,000 years ago? Is it possible the people we call "natives" weren't the first North Americans? Did Europeans get here first? Maybe. Kennewick Man is one of several human skeletons found in North America that are around 10,000 years old and that don't look like North American aboriginals. And archaeologists have found stone tools in the United States identical to tools found at prehistoric sites in France and Spain.

Human beings are a species of migrants and always have been. Borders, passports, and visas, all devices to restrain migration, are recent inventions. And despite them, individual migrants like Dave Lu keep finding ways to move from one part of the world to another.

Every nation was founded by people who came from else-where, often displacing existing populations. This historical fact is easily overlooked by Canadians, indoctrinated as they have been with the notion that Canada is a "nation of immi-grants" and that this sets non-aboriginal Canadians apart from aboriginal Canadians and from Europeans living in Europe. Everyone on the planet – including Dave Lu's parents in Liu Zhai, including Queen Elizabeth, including Matthew Coon Come, national chief of the Assembly of First Nations – is descended from an immigrant.

What do we mean when we say Canada is a nation of immi-grants – unlike European, Asian, or African countries, which we say are not? Perhaps we mean that the Americas, like Australia and New Zealand, were settled (by non-aboriginals) relatively recently. Europeans established permanent settlements in Canada 400 years ago, 1,300 years after the Anglo-Saxons first arrived in Britain. And in its early history Canada recruited immigrants as part of an organized effort of nation-building. The Anglo-Saxons who invaded Celtic Britain, by contrast, were uninvited migrants.

A senior bureaucrat in the immigration department once told me he had to train all new English-Canadian immigration ministers not to use "nation of immigrants" while in Quebec "because it doesn't play well there." Québécois think of them-selves as a nation of Québécois, not as a nation of immigrants. Montreal has long been a magnet for immigrants, but the rest of the province hasn't. So it seems diversity, more than recent arrival, is what "nation of immigrants" refers to. The phrase is a way of saying that English-speaking Canada, unlike Quebec or England, lacks a dominant ethnicity.

Ethnicity is a cultural phenomenon rather than a racial one. There is no such thing as a Canadian race, but there is no such thing as an English, French, or German race either. A person has German ethnicity if he or she shares language and other cultural attributes with other Germans and feels a sense of sol-idarity with them. Many Canadians, especially immigrants and their children (second-generation Canadians), identify them-selves as having some non-Canadian ethnicity while being Canadian at the same time. This is normal and in no way dis-tinctively Canadian.

On the other hand, millions of Canadians do not identify with the ethnicity of their ancestors. Their parents may have had different ethnic backgrounds, thus diluting the ethnicity of their children. They themselves may be married to someone of a different ethnic background. If they are third-generation Canadians, they probably do not speak the ancestral language unless their ancestors spoke English. Most of their social connections are to other Canadians of a wide variety of back-grounds who speak Canadian English and whose cultural touch-stones are Canadian and global.

Such people have Canadian ethnicity. They have it even though the Liberal government and the ideologues of multi-culturalism wish they didn't, for the doctrine of multicultural-ism states that there is no such thing. Increasingly, however, Canadians reject this doctrine and with it the government's per-verse attempt to deny Canadians their identity. That is why many insist on describing their ethnicity as "Canadian" when they fill out census forms.

Maybe it's time to retire the "nation of immigrants" chest-nut. There are good reasons for doing so. The phrase embodies the idea, beloved of multiculturalists, that all non-native Canadians are somehow immigrants. But this idea robs the word of its meaning. If we can't even agree on the meaning of "immi-grant," how can we discuss immigration policy? All humans are descended from immigrants, so if the definition of immigrant is broadened to mean "descendant of an immigrant," the word becomes synonymous with "human" and no longer useful.

An immigrant is someone born in one country who lives in another. By this definition, Canada is not a nation of immi-grants at all. It's a nation mainly of non-immigrants; 83 percent of Canadians were born in Canada. And if that's not reason enough for giving the phrase "nation of immigrants" a rest, consider that, like "racist," it's frequently used to squelch debate and avoid thought.

Kean Bhatacharya came to Canada from India via Britain; he's a retired Toronto accountant with a deep interest in immi-gration policy. His studies have led him to question current poli-cies. As a loyal Canadian, he would like to see them changed. What's frustrating for Bhatacharya is that no political vehicle for change exists. His views, though they represent those of a majority of Canadians, are ignored by politicians. The Canadian Alliance Party has attacked abuse of the refugee system, but no party questions the excessive numbers of immigrants or the government's preference for unskilled ones.

In 2001 Bhatacharya had the idea that Joe Clark, as leader of a Progressive Conservative Party reduced to a sliver of its former self, might be interested in formulating a new approach to what should be an important issue, an approach that might give many Canadians a reason to support his party rather than the Liberals. He wrote Clark asking why Canada should have twice as much immigration per capita as the United States and what Clark thought about the contribution of immigration-fuelled population growth to worsening pollution and traffic gridlock in Toronto.

"Canada is a country of immigrants," Clark wrote back, as if that settled the matter. None of Bhatacharya's thoughtful questions were addressed. Instead, the Tory leader rattled off a string of platitudes that might have come directly out of a Liberal minister's briefing book. Orwell would have understood. Questioning immigration policy, even policy as unfathomable as that of the Chrétien government, is simply "not done" in Canada. In this environment even an opposition party leader, who has everything to gain from opposing an unpopular government policy, is cowed into conformity.

A hundred years ago, when the prairies were settled, immigration had a readily understandable national purpose: to attract farmers who would turn western Canada into the breadbasket of the world. By the end of the 19th century most of the farmland in the United States had already been settled, whereas vast amounts in Canada remained untouched. Because wheat prices were high, it was in Canada's economic interest to open up the prairies and compete with the Americans on world markets.

Clifford Sifton, minister of the interior in Wilfrid Laurier's government, was in charge of recruiting new settlers. The government mounted an aggressive advertising campaign to get people to accept Canada's offer of free land. The campaign emphasized the desirability of the prairies as a place to live; the word "cold" was never mentioned in government pamphlets, which referred to the winters as "invigorating." When an Irish newspaper, unimpressed by this propaganda, called Manitoba "a kind of Siberia," Sifton tried to ban the publication of Manitoba winter temperatures.

The recruitment campaign was a huge success. Immigration rose from 22,000 in 1897 to its all-time high of 401,000 in 1913. The Sifton immigration explosion ended abruptly – the inflow of newcomers was down to 37,000 by 1915 – and didn't do much to raise the overall population, since almost as many eastern Canadians were emigrating to the United States at the time. But it was a turning point in the immigration history of Canada, because it implanted the image in the Canadian consciousness of immigration as a vital nation-building tool and because it marked the beginning of Canadian diversity. Although most of the 2.5 million immigrants who arrived between 1896 and 1914 were English-speaking, the influx included many Germans, Jews, Russians, Ukrainians, Poles, Hungarians, and Scandinavians.

Sifton also invented the concept of selecting immigrants most likely to do well in Canada. That was why he tried to attract successful farmers from the United States and why, over the objections of some Canadians, he recruited people from eastern Europe. "I think a stalwart peasant in a sheepskin coat born of the soil," he said, "whose forefathers have been farmers for ten generations, with a stout wife and a half dozen children, is good quality."

These seemed like good selection criteria for prairie pioneers. The ability to speak English was not important; nor was education. Today's immigrants, by contrast, must make their way in a complex urban environment. The evidence is conclusive that the ability to speak one of Canada's two official languages is essential for successful integration. And few decent jobs exist for people without at least a high school education. It would probably amaze Sifton, the originator of selective immigration, that Canada in 2002 makes neither language nor education a requirement for most of its immigrants.

The memory of the vast tide of newcomers that arrived at the turn of the 20th century may be another reason why the "nation of immigrants" concept is enduring. In fact, the Sifton interlude was an anomaly. For most of its history, Canada, like every other country, has depended on natural increase (excess of births over deaths), not immigration, to fuel population growth. Of course, as in every other country, it required a founding core of migrants to start the process. The original Canadian settlers were fruitful and they multiplied. The 70,000 people who lived in New France (Quebec) in 1750 were descended from fewer than 10,000 original immigrants.

Canada's population kept growing even when large numbers of Canadians were moving south in search of economic opportunities. During the 30 years that followed Confederation in 1867, 180,000 more people left the country as emigrants than arrived as immigrants. During that period the Canadian population grew by 1.8 million.

The 20th century was also a period of natural population growth. From 1901 to 1996, 12 million immigrants came and 6 million people left, leaving a net gain from immigration of 6 million. That number represents only about one-fifth of Canada's total population growth during the period. Immigration, then, was not the key factor in the expansion of Canada's population, but the success of the Sifton project rightly made it seem a vital nation-building tool, as important as the building of the transcontinental railways and the imposition of tariffs to protect Canadian industry.

For most of the 20th century, immigration was seen as something Canada could use as needed, rather than as a permanent program. In the 1930s, when Canada was suffering devastating unemployment, immigration was all but cut off.

Another major difference between the old immigration

system and today's was that, until 1962, race was an important criterion. The Immigration Act of 1910 gave the government the right to deny entry to people "belonging to any race deemed unsuited to the climate or requirements of Canada." Revisions to the Immigration Act in 1919 included the imposition of a literacy test for all immigrants. Remarkably, this was done at a time when Canada had plenty of jobs for illiterate people.

The new immigration law also allowed the government to designate certain countries as preferred providers of immigrants. These included the United States and the white countries of the Commonwealth. People from these countries faced few impediments to entry. There were more regulations for Europeans, but they too could come as independent immigrants. People from non-white regions, however, could get into Canada only if they had a relative already in the country to sponsor them.

This was an unabashed "white Canada" policy, and it was reaffirmed after World War II by Prime Minister William Lyon Mackenzie King. "Large-scale immigration from the Orient would change the fundamental composition of the Canadian population," he said in a statement to the House of Commons in 1947. By 1962, attitudes were changing. The Conservative government led by John Diefenbaker got rid of regulations favouring immigrants from Britain, the United States, and France and restricting ones from Asia.

It wasn't until the 1990s that immigration became more important than natural increase in population growth. The shift came about because immigration levels were increasing at the same time as the reproductive years of the baby boomers were coming to a close. In 1996, for example, there were, as always, more births than deaths in Canada – 154,300 more – but net migration (immigration minus emigration) was higher, at 184,400.

These numbers reflect two global demographic phenomena of huge importance. One is the decline of fertility in the industrialized countries, a result of aging populations and a preference for small families. The other is rapid population growth in the poor countries, creating a surge in people wanting to move to the West. By some estimates, as many as 100 million people are currently trying, or planning to try, to get from poor countries to rich ones.

The demographics of the planet, then, are utterly different at the beginning of the 21st century than they were at the start of the 20th. Back then, a global population of 1.7 billion was distributed about evenly between the industrialized countries and the underdeveloped ones. Now, of a world population of more than 6 billion, five times as many live in the poor countries as in the rich ones.

One hundred years ago, the only way to move from one part of the globe to another was by ship, a trip that could take many weeks. With the advent of mass air travel, that trip is accomplished in hours. A hundred years ago, the fastest communication was by letter, which took weeks to get from Russia or China to Canada. Today, of course, telephone and e-mail allow instantaneous communication. And television programs and movies, many of them produced in the United States, give struggling families in poor countries tantalizing visions of the easier, richer life available in rich ones.

This combination of population imbalance, rapid transportation, and instant communications explains why migration pressures today are so powerful. These trends not only increase the numbers of people wanting to move, they intensify the desire to move. And they do more than that. They change the very nature of migration. Modern transportation and communications make migration less permanent than it once was and separation from the homeland less complete.

The waves of immigrants that arrived on the prairies early in the 20th century were quickly cut off from the old country. That doesn't happen to today's immigrants; many maintain intimate links to their homelands. Some own businesses in their native countries and others are involved in politics. None of this is unique to immigrants in Canada although only Canada, through its policy of official multiculturalism, actually encourages newcomers to cling to their original identities rather than fully embrace the identity of their new home.

Even without official multiculturalism, Canada would be part of an emerging world in which many people do not feel uniquely tied to one country. Kenichi Ohmae, the Japanese business guru, has described this world as a "genuinely cross-border civilization." The American political scientist Stanley Hoffmann writes of "a global society in which states [are] no longer the only or even the essential players." Global organizations – the Roman Catholic Church, the Rothschild banking network, the Mafia – are hardly new, but global society is far more developed and integrated than ever before. Investors can move money instantly from one country to another, affecting local currencies. Businesses of all sorts operate internationally. Our world is made up of thousands of international organizations and hundreds of millions of interpersonal links. E-mail has created countless "virtual communities" of people with similar interests.

In this environment, it is not surprising that SUCCESS, an organization serving Vancouver's Chinese community, has a special program to deal with the stresses in families headed by "astronauts," people who travel between Vancouver and Hong Kong. In light of Ohmae's thesis, are astronauts really immigrants to Canada? "The countries from which these uprooted people are independently setting out are traditional, politically defined nation states," he writes in *The End of the Nation State*. "The country to which they are all migrating . . . is the global economy of the borderless world."

The borderless world is reflected in the attitudes of recent migrants like Dave Lu. Previous generations of Chinese came to Canada to stay; some of British Columbia's oldest families are of Chinese origin. Today's new arrivals are far less likely to view their new home as permanent. Lu says that many educated Chinese of his generation see going abroad as a career move, not a commitment. He himself admires Canada and loves living on the West Coast. Would he go back to China? "Maybe. But I have to stay here at least three years. I want to get English, to get work experience, and to make connections."

Some 93 countries, including Canada, have accommodated the new global society by authorizing dual citizenship, a trend that pleases some but worries others. "Think of it as a right of free association," Peter Spiro, a law professor at Hofstra University, in Hempstead, New York, told *Investor's Business Daily*. "We would all abhor a rule under which we were not allowed to join other civic forms of association. A rule against dual citizenship is that kind of rule."

But dual citizenship, by definition, amounts to divided loyalty. It may not pose a problem if it applies to only a few. But what happens when a hefty percentage of the population is made up of dual citizens? "No country, and especially no democracy, can afford to have large numbers of citizens with shallow civic and national attachments," argues Stanley Renshon, a professor of political science at City University of New York, who has made a study of the subject. He points to a 1997 survey of Muslims in Los Angeles in which 80 percent said they owed their first allegiance to a country other than the United States.

It's hardly surprising that these people would have divided loyalties. We live, after all, in a world in which you can become an immigrant while retaining intimate links to the homeland. We're heading down a new road and, as the unease over dual citizenship indicates, it's not clear where that road is taking us. As the industrialized countries adapt tentatively to this new world, they're struggling to figure out how international migration fits into it.

Certainly we need to distinguish between individual migration and mass migration, between Dave Lu, who arrived at Vancouver International Airport after having his application to emigrate approved, and the boatloads of unskilled Chinese migrants who attempted in 1999 to enter Canada illegally.

Increasingly, nations have shown a willingness to liberalize the movement of people like Lu while closing the doors on the unwanted masses. In Europe, for example, citizens of European Union countries can reside in any member country. And why not? It's a win-win scenario. The German company that obtains the services of the French citizen with precisely the skills it needs obviously benefits. So does the French citizen, who finds in Germany the professional setting where her talents are best rewarded. This system works because the standards of living in European Union countries are roughly equal. There's no economic incentive for masses of French people to move to Germany, or vice versa.

There is, of course, every reason for masses of Africans or eastern Europeans to move to western Europe, which is why immigration from those areas is tightly controlled. People from poor countries have everything to gain from trying to get into rich ones. Small wonder that illegal immigration is on the increase all over the world. The pressure is especially intense where poor nations abut rich ones – at the U.S.-Mexico border, for instance, where more than 1.5 million people are arrested annually trying to enter the United States illegally. Another such juxtaposition is the Mediterranean Sea, which separates Africa from Europe. Illegal immigrants in the European Union countries have multiplied from about 50,000 in 1993 to an estimated 500,000 in 1999. Such statistics help explain the rise of political movements opposed to immigration.

The industrialized countries all face the same dilemma. Except for the United States, they have below-replacement fertility; eventually, in the absence of immigration or a rebound in fertility, they will experience declining populations. These countries must decide whether to live with population decline or allow enough immigration to provide population stability.

The traditional immigrant-receiving countries – Canada, the United States, and Australia – have already made that decision. All three have much younger populations than Europe and Japan, and all three have generous immigration programs; as a result, they have no worries about population decline. The same is not true of many of the western European countries, or of Japan. These are older societies with low fertility and generally restrictive immigration policies.

Proponents of open immigration ask why, in a world in which goods are more freely and easily traded than ever, these nations put up barriers to people, especially when they could benefit from an injection of young blood. Humans, remember, have always been migrants by nature; why not accept that fact and completely knock down the rickety, costly fences we call borders? Because, while the industrialized countries probably do need to add people from outside their exclusive club, they don't have room for all 100 million who are eager to emigrate. That's why, even in a global society, borders will have a future for a long time to come.

CHAPTER THREE

THE LONGEST UNDEFENDED BORDER

THREE DAYS AFTER THE TERRORIST ATTACKS IN MANHATTAN and Washington, the president of a Toronto manufacturing company received a letter from an important customer in North Carolina. The customer acknowledged the Canadian executive's offer to help any American customers stranded in Canada because of the diversion of air traffic bound for the United States. He added: "Last night I was shocked to learn from news accounts that your country has no laws against belonging to known terrorist groups, nor any laws against contributing funds to those groups. If this is true . . . Canadian companies we have relationships with can expect no further orders from my company until this is rectified."

What the American businessman had heard on television and read in the *Wall Street Journal* was true. At the time, Canada had no anti-terrorism legislation. Moreover, it allowed refugee claimants, including people who had arrived with false documents or no documents at all, to roam freely within its borders. Indeed, we encouraged such people to come by approving a higher percentage of refugee claims than any other country in the world, and by offering claimants free legal aid, health and dental care, and other social benefits. Even when illegal immigrants were identified as terrorists, Canada rarely got rid of them because government-funded refugee lawyers merrily exploited an almost endless maze of legal barriers to deportation.

After the attacks, there was talk of creating a security perimeter around the United States and Canada. This notion grew out of the idea that the two countries would exert strict control over who was allowed to gain access to their part of the North American continent. Once inside North America, anyone, foreigner or citizen, could move freely across the U.S.-Canada border.

There were two problems with this idea. One was that the Canadian immigration and refugee systems were in such disarray that American security would be compromised if border controls were removed. The other was that the U.S. system was also a mess; Canadian security, too, would be at risk if Canada stopped checking people entering from the south.

Through October 2001, erroneous reports that the hijackers had entered from Canada were accompanied by a wave of descriptions in American media about the laxness of Canada's immigration system. The coverage tended to leave out, or gloss over, the fact that far more people cross illegally into the United States from Mexico than from Canada, and that millions of people who entered the United States legally as visitors or students have stayed on illegally. This group included many of the September 11 hijackers. It was America's fault, not Canada's, that, at the end of 2001, 8 million foreigners were in the United States illegally, some 5 million Mexicans and 3 million other people. Nevertheless, it was Canada – especially our inept system for dealing with refugee claimants – that had captured the Americans' attention. Their once-friendly northern neighbours suddenly represented a grave security risk.

Borders define countries. They're what gives a country the

right to decide who gets in. If a country loses the ability to make that decision, if it loses control of its borders, then its sovereignty – its very existence as an independent nation – is threatened. Canada shares a border with only one country, and it happens to be the most powerful in the world. The United States has almost 10 times the population of Canada, and it wields massive military, economic, and cultural power. When the power relationship between neighbouring countries is so unbalanced, the border becomes all the more critical. For Canada, the border allows us to keep our distance from the United States. It allows us to let in the American stuff we want – fast-food restaurants, for example, and movies – and keep out what we don't, such as for-profit health care and guns.

Americans, especially of late, see the border differently. For people like the angry businessman in North Carolina, the border is about protection from foreign zealots who want to kill them. If Canada was going to admit dangerous people, then the United States was going to have to protect itself by securing its 8,900-kilometre border with Canada. Which is why, in the wake of the terrorist attacks, the U.S. government sent National Guard troops and helicopters to defend what had been the world's longest undefended border.

Armed soldiers were an extraordinary sight to Canadians. The border had long been a source of pride, symbolized by the Peace Arch that has stood for more than 80 years at the boundary between Douglas, British Columbia, and Blaine, Washington. Douglas-Blaine is one of four major crossings (the other three are in Ontario) that accommodate 70 percent of traffic between the countries. These crossings, with their never-ending streams of cars and trucks, are the rivers on which flow the most intense two-way trade in the world.

On average, a truck crosses the border every three seconds. As of the end of 2001, this trade was worth $1.4 billion a day to Canada. Canada is also the biggest customer of the United

States, receiving 25 percent of everything the Americans export. Some 200 million people cross the border every year, including many thousands who live in border communities and cross almost daily to work or shop.

Sparsely populated places like Jamison Line, New York, or North Portal, Saskatchewan, are what many Canadians think of when they hear "the world's longest undefended border." In various villages, the border cuts through a public library, factories, even someone's bedroom. At Jamison Line, only about 20 vehicles a day cross the border. Before September 11, the crossing was staffed only eight hours a day. At other times, people were directed by a sign to another entry post a short drive away. The honour system prevailed and nothing prevented anyone from entering the United States illegally. Since September 11, the post has been staffed 24 hours a day.

North Portal is one of those places where the border is an abstraction. The 200 people who live there and in adjoining Portal, North Dakota, form a single community, attend the same clubs and churches, eat at the same restaurants. They play at a golf club where, on the ninth hole, you tee off in Canada and putt out in the United States. Even people crossing from North Portal to Portal got tougher checks after September 11. For them, the delays were an inconvenience.

The slowdowns of truck traffic at the big four crossings were considerably more than that. Had they continued, the Canadian economy would have been devastated. The Ambassador Bridge, linking Windsor and Detroit, is the world's busiest land-border crossing, accommodating 3.5 million trucks in 1999. It's the vital link in the integrated automaking industry that powers the economies of both Michigan and Ontario. After September 11, truckers waited 15 hours or more while U.S. inspectors scoured their vehicles for terrorists, explosives, or biological weapons. Some Canadian assembly plants had to shut down until the delays eased. More than a month later, delays of an hour or more were still routine.

Canada's economy is too dependent on easy access to the United States to tolerate such delays indefinitely. Parts manufacturers in southern Ontario make deliveries to plants in Michigan all day long on a just-in-time basis. If the trucks can't cross swiftly, the system breaks down. That's why the logic of a U.S.-Canada perimeter, with joint control over who gets in, makes sense. Once inside the perimeter, crossing into the United States from Canada would be like crossing from Germany to Belgium. You glance at a sign announcing you've changed countries, but you don't even need to slow down.

Given that Canada's economic well-being depends on trade with the United States, and given the Americans' overwhelming preoccupation with security, the notion of a common perimeter seems almost irresistible. Each side gets what it wants: the Canadians get barrier-free access to the American market, while the Americans get to feel safer.

Paul Cellucci, the U.S. ambassador to Ottawa, was pushing the perimeter idea even before September 11. But the Canadians were resisting. Many Canadians, including members of the Liberal cabinet and caucus, thought too much cooperation threatened our independence. We were already in a military alliance with the United States through NATO and NORAD; we had troops in Afghanistan under U.S. command; on the trade front, we were under relentless pressure to change economic policies the Americans didn't like (such as our system of granting logging licences or the export monopoly enjoyed by the Canadian Wheat Board). And now we were supposed to consider a common perimeter, which would mean changing our immigration and refugee policies to suit the Americans? How much integration could Canada tolerate without fatally compromising its sovereignty?

Unspoken, however, was the real reason for the Liberals' unease: a North American perimeter threatened their ability to run the immigration program for political gain. The Americans might insist that Canada reduce its annual intake to a more manageable number so that all new immigrants could be thoroughly checked and security risks weeded out. This would weaken the Liberals' ability to replenish the ethnic blocs.

The United States could also be expected to insist that Canada dump its Immigration and Refugee Board in favour of a professional tribunal capable of applying the Geneva Convention; such a tribunal would be less likely to allow dangerous individuals to stay in North America. But losing the IRB would deprive the Liberals of scores of $100,000-a-year jobs for party supporters and defeated candidates. Harmonization of policies was needed, Ambassador Cellucci said, to "establish a North American perimeter that would apply more rigorous controls for people landing from overseas . . . We need to defend the people of North America from these kinds of vicious attacks." No like statements were uttered by Canadian officials.

Both the United States and Canada take pride in being open, pluralistic societies. The chief lesson of September 11 is that this openness can be used against us. Both countries were vulnerable in part because they operated generous immigration programs that made it easy for dangerous people to get in and then blend in. Changes are called for, but the idea of eliminating border controls raises two crucial questions. Does the United States, if it opens its border to Canada, have anything to fear from Canadian immigration policy? Yes, indeed. And does Canada, if it opens its border to the United States, have anything to fear from U.S. immigration policy? Yes again.

WHY THE UNITED STATES SHOULD FEAR CANADA

In February 2002, Canada's Immigration and Refugee Board granted refugee status to Tafari Rennock, a Jamaican who had been deported from the United States for criminal offences. Canada is the only country where Rennock could have been classified a Geneva Convention refugee, because the IRB is the only refugee tribunal that considers the United States a refugee-producing country. Thanks to the IRB, Canada gets to keep a man whose criminal record includes sexual assault, drug trafficking, and robbery. If agreement on a joint perimeter were reached and border controls between Canada and the United States eliminated, Tafari Rennock would be free to cross back into the States.

If the United States didn't have border controls, Won Pil Park also could have gone there. He's a South Korean ordered deported from Canada in 1995 for killing a Hamilton, Ontario, teenager in an incident of road rage. An IRB adjudicator granted him a stay of deportation. This enabled him to rape a young Japanese student, an employee in his Hamilton restaurant, in her apartment. In the process, he gave her a sexually transmitted disease. Daniele D'Ignazio, the IRB adjudicator who allowed Park to stay despite the deportation order, explained that it would be an "undue hardship" to separate him from his family, who are Canadian citizens. There is no possibility the United States will remove barriers to entry at its border with Canada if it means leaving American citizens at the mercy of the criminals and other undesirables unleashed on Canadian society by the IRB, an organization of spectacular incompetence.

Much was heard after September 11 of Canada's determination to beef up its security. True, the Liberal government did take action. It replaced some of the money it had previously cut from the budgets of the military and CSIS. It passed an anti-terrorism law that gave police expanded powers, including the power to detain terrorist suspects without a warrant. And it began preparing for terrorist attacks. In February 2002, for example, U.S. and Canadian counter-intelligence officials conducted a simulation of a mass anthrax attack on Seattle and Vancouver.

But nothing was done to address the root causes of Canada's vulnerability to terrorism: an immigration program that lets in more people than is consistent with public safety, and a refugee system that allows known criminals and terrorists and unidentified people from all over the world to roam freely in Canada.

In the aftermath of September 11, it was business as usual at the IRB. Some 2,500 people from terrorist-producing countries made refugee claims in Canada during the last four months of 2001. Most were released pending hearings of their claims.

In late 2001, *The West Wing*, the popular TV show about a fictional U.S. president and his staff, aired an episode inspired by the events of September 11. Reference was made to terrorists who had entered the United States from Canada by crossing the "Ontario-Vermont" border. Liberal cabinet members and other defenders of Canadian immigration policy were outraged. Not only had none of the September terrorists entered the United States from Canada, but Ontario and Vermont do not share a border.

Implicit in the Liberals' reaction was the suggestion that no terrorist threat emanates from Canada. The suggestion is self-serving and deceitful. Canada is indeed a terrorist threat, both to itself and to its neighbours, and this threat was documented long before September 11.

In 1998 Ward Elcock, director of the Canadian Security Intelligence Service, told a Canadian Senate committee that "there are more international terrorist groups active here than in any country in the world," perhaps with the exception of the United States. CSIS, he said, was investigating 50 organizations and 350 individuals suspected of being terrorists. The organizations included Hezbollah and other Shiite Islamic terrorist organizations; several Sunni Islamic extremist groups, including Hamas; the Irish Republican Army; the Tamil Tigers; the Kurdistan Workers' Party; and all the major Sikh terrorist groups.

In May 2000, CSIS issued a report entitled *International Terrorism: The Threat to Canada*. The report pointed out that Canada had signed a dozen international conventions on combatting terrorism yet "has been a frequent destination for international terrorists and their supporters." These organizations are part of the "global society" described in chapter 2. They are in communication with their confederates in other countries, and their international efforts are coordinated. In February 1999, Abdullah Ocalan, leader of the Kurdistan Workers' Party (PKK), was arrested in Kenya; the next day, PKK supporters staged a violent riot in Montreal. The day after that, they did the same in Ottawa. Several policemen were injured; one lost an eye and another was set afire by a Molotov cocktail.

Sikh terrorists, campaigning for a separate homeland in Punjab, are active in Canada. Inderjit Singh Reyat, a Sikh extremist living in British Columbia, is affiliated with the terrorist organization Babbar Khalsa. He was convicted of building the suitcase bomb that killed two baggage handlers at Tokyo's Narita Airport in 1985. The bomb had been placed in a suitcase loaded onto a Canadian plane leaving Vancouver on the same day as the Air India bombing that killed 329 people over the Atlantic.

Kim Bolan, a reporter for the *Vancouver Sun*, started investigating Sikh extremists after the 1985 bombings. In 1997, after a series of articles about a school linked to suspects in the bombing, she received her first death threat. "You stop or you will die," it said. The letter also threatened the life of Tara Singh Hayer, a contact of Bolan's and publisher of the *Indo-Canadian Times*, a Punjabi-language newspaper that opposed the extremists. Hayer had been shot nine years earlier and was confined to a wheelchair. A few months later, a shot was fired late at night outside Bolan's house, and in November 1998, Tara Singh Hayer was shot dead in his garage.

By February 1999, the rhetoric by Sikh extremists against Bolan had become so vicious that the Vancouver police decided she needed protection. She and members of her family were escorted everywhere. Bodyguards accompanied her to speaking engagements in Los Angeles and New York.

Cheerleaders for Canada's immigration program, in the federal government and outside it, claim that no terrorist activity in Canada is tied to immigration. "There is no connection between immigration and violence," states the Web site of the Canadian Council for Refugees, a lobby group for refugee claimants and their lawyers. This is denial of the obvious. A terrorist is someone who attacks innocent civilians in the name of a political cause. The Sikh extremists who terrorized Hayer and Bolan are in Canada because Canada, through its immigration and refugee program, let them in.

The IRB routinely grants refugee status to Sikh opponents of the Indian government. "You give them refugee status and we give them visas," the Indian consulate in Vancouver once told Des Verma, an Indian-born former member of the IRB. The consulate meant that Sikh separatists, having obtained refugee status in Canada, often return to the very place they claimed they had to flee – tantamount to an admission that the refugee claim was a lie.

Though the Canadian government has the right to ask the IRB to "vacate" (nullify) refugee status, it almost never does. As a result, Canada is home to many Sikh refugees who, by returning to India on visits, acknowledge that they obtained such status by fraud. Some are terrorists. Why would the Americans allow such people unimpeded access to their country? So they could attack law-abiding American Sikhs and terrorize American journalists?

Canada's status as a hotbed of terrorist activity has not gone unnoticed outside the country. In January 2000, Steve Emerson testified at a U.S. House of Representatives hearing on the subject of international terrorism and immigration policy. Emerson, a former journalist, runs a counter-terrorism institute in Washington. "For a number of reasons, Canada is an attractive venue for terrorists," he told the U.S. politicians. "Long borders and coastlines offer many points of entry, which can facilitate movement to and from various sites around the world, particularly the U.S. As a wealthy industrial society, Canada is an excellent location in which to raise money in the name of causes abroad. The nation accepts large numbers of immigrants and refugees, and consequently has significant émigré communities, which can be a source of haven and support."

Emerson described the case of Mohammed Hussein al-Husseini, who arrived in Canada in 1991 without documents and was awarded refugee status by the IRB. Though he claimed to be fleeing persecution in Lebanon, he went back there after getting his refugee documents, which he also used to travel to the United States. On learning that al-Husseini was a member of Hezbollah, the immigration department sought to deport him. In interviews, he described the support the terrorist organization had received from the Canadian Islamic community. He also provided a video of potential Canadian targets taken by Hezbollah members in Canada. The video had been sent back to headquarters in Lebanon in case Hezbollah decided to target Canada.

What, exactly, do terrorist organizations do in Canada? According to Emerson, they provide logistical support to operations in other countries by obtaining weapons and equipment to be shipped abroad. They raise money and produce propaganda. They intimidate and manipulate Canadian ethnic communities to support their causes. They provide a safe haven for terrorists. (As an example, Emerson named Hani Al-Sayegh, accused of participating in a 1996 bombing in Saudi Arabia that killed 19 Americans. Shortly after the bombing, he arrived in Canada from Kuwait.) And they use Canada as a base to direct terrorism in other countries. For some Sikh groups, Emerson said, Canada is headquarters.

The country most likely to be victimized by Canadian-based terrorists is the United States. In his 1998 Canadian Senate appearance, CSIS director Elcock said transit of terrorists to and from the States is an important activity of terrorist organizations in Canada. Gazi Ibrahim Abu Mezer, for example, used Canada as his entry to North America before moving on to the United States. A Palestinian, Abu Mezer arrived in Canada in 1993 on a student visa. Nobody checked his background. If they had, they might have discovered that he had been held on security charges by Israeli authorities who believed he was linked to the terrorist organization Hamas.

In Canada he was arrested twice for minor offences. He applied for a visa to the United States and was rejected. The U.S. Immigration and Naturalization Service (INS) twice caught him trying to sneak across remote sections of the border between British Columbia and Washington State. Both times, he was sent back to Canada. The third time he was arrested, he was in the United States, boarding a bus in Bellingham, near the Canadian border.

Abu Mezer claimed asylum. The INS usually detains undocumented asylum-seekers, but in areas that have many illegal immigrants and not enough jail space, claimants are released. Abu Mezer went to Brooklyn. There he began building pipe bombs intended to blow up a subway station. Acting on a tip from one of his roommates, police arrested him. As the case illustrates, the Americans have enough problems dealing with inadequacies in their own immigration and refugee system without the further danger that would result from removing the barriers at the Canadian border.

The case of another Muslim, Nabil Al-Marabh, shows that the Canadians can't be relied upon to keep people with known terrorist connections out of circulation. Al-Marabh, who made a refugee claim in Canada in 1994, was identified as an al-Qaeda agent by Raed Hijazi, who confessed to conspiring to blow up tourist sites in Jordan. Nevertheless, Al-Marabh was able to move back and forth between Canada and the United States. For a time he worked as a cab driver in Boston.

In June 2001, the Americans caught him trying to sneak into the United States in a tractor-trailer, carrying a false passport. They returned him to Canada where he was released on bail. He got back in and was arrested in Chicago on September 19, 2001, suspected of involvement in the September 11 assault.

"Security at the Canadian border is woefully inadequate.

There's no question that terrorists could be sneaking in right now," Mark Krikorian said in a post–September 11 interview in the *Boston Globe*. Krikorian is executive director of the Center for Immigration Studies, a Washington-based think tank, and an authority on international immigration policy. "Terrorists from all over the world have been using Canada's asylum system," he said. "You can come in [to Canada] with no documents, or fake documents, and say you want asylum and they let you in. We [the United States] detain large numbers of asylum seekers. They don't."

The Chrétien government's attitude to the security risks is that of courtiers to the emperor with no clothes: just say over and over that the emperor is handsomely dressed. There seems to have been a deliberate attempt by the government to pretend that the Air India bombing wasn't really Canadian-based terrorism, even though the bomb-laden plane took off from Canada. Murders in Sri Lanka of civilians by suicide bombers and other terrorists were not recognized as Canadian-based terrorism despite the Sri Lankan government's assertion that much of the money for these actions was raised in Canada.

The government also tends to downplay the Canadian Security Intelligence Service's blunt portrayal of Canada as a hub of terrorist activity. Even as it defended its anti-terrorism bill from critics who claimed the terrorist threat was exaggerated, the government rarely made mention of the 50 terrorist organizations operating in Canada. Harris, the former CSIS chief of strategic planning, says the estimate of 50 is conservative because it is a couple of years old. "Any recognizable terrorist group in the world is here," he says. "After the United States, we are the biggest host of terrorist organizations in the world."

In October 2001, an Israeli security publication, *Debka File*, citing European intelligence sources, said that al-Qaeda was maintaining command and logistics posts in Vancouver and Toronto, to be used to launch a new wave of attacks against the United States. The editor of *Debka File*, Shamis Giora, said that the presence of key al-Qaeda personnel in Canada was "general knowledge" among European intelligence agencies.

The disappearance from Montreal in January 2002 of two Tunisian immigrants seemed to give credence to this report. One of them, Al Rauf bin Al Habib bin Yousef al-Jiddi, appeared in a martyrdom video salvaged from the ruins of a home in Kabul that had belonged to one of Osama bin Laden's top lieutenants. In the video, al-Jiddi and four other men were seen brandishing assault rifles and pledging "war against the infidels." The United States declared that the two Canadian citizens were al-Qaeda terrorists bent on suicide missions and launched a manhunt for them.

Whether or not the Israeli report was fully accurate, there is no doubt Canada faces a new reality and little evidence that Canadians or their government fully appreciate it. Islamic terrorism is, to a North American, frighteningly different from IRA or Kurdish or Tamil terrorism: its targets are in North America. "This is a revolutionary shift in the terrorist threat that Canada faces, and Canadians are so far refusing to recognize its scale and nature," says Harris. "You would almost imagine that our lives were not at stake."

Defenders of Canada point out that the majority of the millions of people crossing into the United States from Canada annually are harmless. This is not reassuring: it took only 19 hijackers and probably a few support personnel on the ground to mount the devastating attack. No country can keep dangerous people from gaining access to its territory, but every country should make all reasonable efforts to minimize the chances of dangerous people getting in. Canada clearly does not do that. Not only does our immigration program leave us vulnerable to terrorism, it leaves us vulnerable to criminals. And because we are vulnerable, so are the Americans. In a comprehensive report on international crime in 2000, the U.S. National Security Council had this to say about Canada:

The United States faces a growing threat from Chinese organized crime groups that are using Canada as a base from which to conduct criminal activities that impact our country. Members of ethnic Chinese criminal groups from China, Hong Kong, Taiwan, and Macau have exploited Ottawa's immigration policies and entrepreneur program to enter the country and become Canadian residents, which makes it easier for them to cross into the United States. Canada has become a gateway for Chinese criminal activity directed at the United States, particularly heroin trafficking, credit card fraud, and software piracy.

The two largest Hong Kong triads, 14K and Sun Yee On, increased their presence and made substantial property investments in Canada in the 1990s. Prominent 14K members from Hong Kong and Macau have emigrated to Canada, and Sun Yee On triad members have settled in Toronto, Edmonton, and Vancouver. The 14K, which has a chapter in Toronto, also has been tied to Asian criminal activities in New York and other U.S. cities. Sun Yee On members are involved in trafficking heroin and methamphetamine, as well as alien smuggling, to the United States, where the triad has ties to New York's Tung On Gang.

The most active Asian criminal group operating in Canada, according to the National Security Council report, is the Big Circle Gang. It's responsible for importing a great deal of the Southeast Asian heroin entering Canada – much of which is smuggled into the United States – and is the source of many of the counterfeit credit cards used in North America.

Other criminal organizations are entrenched in Canada. In 2002 the Nathanson Centre for the Study of Organized Crime and Corruption, based at Toronto's York University, issued a report stating that violent ethnic gangs in Canadian cities are linked to terrorist organizations in South Asia. Tamil gangs are connected to the Tamil Tigers in Sri Lanka; Punjabi gangs are linked to violent separatist organizations in India.

The name of one Toronto gang, VVT, is derived from the birthplace of Vellupillai Prabhakaran, leader of the Tigers. VVT, which has attacked refugees in Canada for criticizing the Tigers, collects money for the Sri Lankan terrorists. The explosive mix used by a Tamil gang in Toronto for a car bombing was identical to the mix used by the Tigers. This, said the report, "perhaps casts light on the possibility that members of VVT gangs have been trained in LTTE [Tiger] camps . . . Many proclaim that the criminal gangs and the LTTE are two separate entities, but there occurs a frequent overlap of acts between the LTTE and the gangs which obfuscates the dividing line."

Whereas the Tamil gangs are made up of recent immigrants, the Punjabi gangs are formed by second-generation Sikhs. "Key actors in the criminal scene have also been known to be active in the political scene," said the Nathanson Centre report. Ron Dosanjh, a gang leader, was president of the Vancouver chapter of the International Sikh Youth Federation.

Canada's lackadaisical approach to immigration documents has long been a sore point with the U.S. government. In March 2002, the RCMP began an investigation into a smuggling ring based in Pakistan that was using Canada's IMM 1000 landed immigrant document to smuggle people into Canada and the United States. The investigation became public after a former immigration department staff member alleged that his bosses in Montreal ignored a Pakistani man who informed them about the ring after September 11. According to the Montreal paper *La Presse*, the IMM 1000 forms, which contain no photos and only limited identification data, were illegally obtained and then supplied to people in Pakistan, who paid up to $25,000 to be escorted to North America.

The government sought to portray its new immigration bill, C-11, as toughening Canada's defence against terrorists and criminals. In fact it did just the opposite; it added further levels of appeal. Analyzing the bill, which became law as the Immigration and Refugee Protection Act late in 2001, James Bissett, a former ambassador and former head of the immigration service, wrote in the *Globe and Mail* that it "leaves Canada wide open for easy entry to undesirables. It seems designed to ensure that the bad guys can never be sent home. Does anyone still wonder why our allies doubt Canada's seriousness in the fight against terrorism?"

What had been an irritation to the Americans is now a matter of urgency. Most of the Americans' attention had been directed towards the Mexican border, where about 1.5 million people a year are arrested trying to slip into the States (compared with about 12,000 a year arrested trying to cross from Canada). But the attacks showed that the Canadian border was of greater strategic importance. The key cities that were attacked, New York and Washington, are much closer to Canada than to Mexico. So are such other major economic centres as Chicago and Boston.

Canada wants unimpeded access for its goods. The United States wants security. If Canada wants trade, it has to give the United States security. In February 2002, the two countries clashed over a "smart border" plan to speed up truck travel across the border. This is something Canada badly wants, since 70 percent of its exports are carried by truck.

The idea is that trucks would be sealed at their points of origin and pre-cleared to use fast lanes at the border. But Robert Bonner, the U.S. commissioner of customs, wasn't buying. "We're looking at increased security against terrorists at the border," he told the *New York Times*. "I don't think Canadians are looking at it the same way. There are at least a certain number of al Qaeda terrorists in Canada. One of them could get a job at one of these [Canadian manufacturing] plants and then you may have nuclear material inserted in that truck."

As we've seen, Canada's refugee system has enabled people who want to do horrible things to the United States to gain entry to Canada, and its immigration program allows them to obtain support and anonymity within large ethnic communities. Who could argue that Bonner's fear of Canada isn't well founded? The terrorist organizations dedicated to the defeat of the "Great Satan" are resourceful and fanatical. The attacks on the World Trade Center put downtown Manhattan out of commission for weeks; even a primitive nuclear explosive could put it out of commission for decades.

Canada's immigration program is contrary to the national interest because, among other reasons, it endangers our economic relationship with the United States. Yet the government won't replace the IRB with a competent refugee tribunal, won't detain unidentified refugee claimants, and won't reduce the annual immigration intake to a manageable number. The price for this self-indulgence may well prove to be ever longer and costlier delays for Canadian exports at the U.S. border.

WHY CANADA SHOULD FEAR THE UNITED STATES

Only one country in the world has more terrorist organizations operating inside it than Canada: the United States. That is reason enough for Canada to fear the United States, its porous borders, its immigration industry, and its blundering bureaucrats.

Many Canadians seemed to shrug off the terrorist attacks on the United States as a U.S. problem only, as if Canada might not also become a target of terrorism. There is no excuse for such complacency. Al-Qaeda's Montreal cell, a group that included the convicted millennium bomber Ahmed Ressam, considered placing a bomb in the Outremont district of Montreal because Ressam and his accomplice, Samir Ait Mohamed, had seen orthodox Jews there. The Montreal terrorists, according to the testimony of a U.S. FBI agent who interrogated Ressam, also considered Rue Sainte-Catherine as a target because it is a busy commercial thoroughfare.

During the war in Afghanistan, the *Wall Street Journal* obtained computers containing documents apparently drafted by members of Osama bin Laden's inner circle. These documents described what appeared to be a plan to bomb Israeli diplomatic missions in Canada. Originally, bin Laden's goal in forming al-Qaeda was to overthrow "infidel" Arab governments such as that of Saudi Arabia. But an al-Qaeda defector, Jamal Ahmed al-Fadl, told American officials in 1996 that the goal had been broadened to include not just the United States but all Western governments.

A fatwa issued by al-Qaeda in 1998 and renewed in 2001 called for the killing of Americans and their allies, including Canadians. The fatwa, endorsed by several Islamic terrorist organizations, directs that these enemies be killed whether they are civilians or soldiers.

Canadian soldiers fought against bin Laden in Afghanistan and turned al-Qaeda and Taliban prisoners over to the U.S. forces. Canada shares the secular, democratic values of Western civilization, a civilization that Muslim extremists believe it their religious duty to destroy. Moreover, Canada is an open, liberal society. It is easy to get into Canada and easy to obtain false Canadian documents. Terrorists, as is well known, tend to seek the path of least resistance. That path leads to Canada.

And yet many Canadians do not appear ready to take Osama bin Laden at his word and acknowledge the seriousness of the threat. As the scientist Edward O. Wilson wrote, in *The Future of Life*, the human species is "innately inclined to ignore any distant possibility not yet requiring examination." The attacks on New York and Washington were hardly distant – New York is less than an hour by air from Montreal or Toronto – but they happened there, not here. Until it happens here, many of us simply don't want to think about it.

The major reason Canada should fear the United States is that the States is home to the greatest collection of unidentified illegal immigrants anywhere in the world. The U.S. Census Bureau estimated in 2001 that more than 8 million illegal aliens were living there, including some 115,000 people from terrorist-producing countries in the Middle East.

It is odd that the Americans have focused so much attention on their northern border in the aftermath of the September 11 attacks, since only a small proportion of their illegal immigrants arrived from Canada. About 5 million came across the shorter but more porous Mexican border. As for the rest, most of them entered legally, on visitor, student, or temporary work visas, but failed to go home when the visas expired.

Many Americans have the impression that Canada, because its government is so naive and its immigration program so lax, is more dangerous to them than Mexico. We export people like Ahmed Ressam and Abu Mezer who want to set off big bombs while, so Americans seem to think, the Mexicans send only harmless workers eager to clean American houses and pick American crops at wages below the legal minimum. In fact, bad guys are as likely to get into the United States from Mexico as from Canada. An increasing number of people arrested coming over the Mexican border are what U.S. Border Patrol agents call OTMs, or "other than Mexicans." These include people from the Middle East, Asia, and the former Soviet Union.

The *San Diego Union Tribune* reported, for example, that Mexican immigration agents arrested 41 undocumented Iraqis waiting to cross into the United States just hours after the September 11 attacks. About the same time, 10 Egyptians were arrested near Douglas, Arizona, after paying US$7,000 to be brought from Guatemala to Mexico and then across the border. And 13 Yemeni citizens were arrested near the border shortly after September 11.

A group of U.S. politicians, visiting a Mexican border town in December 2001, found that travel documents were readily available. "We asked the first person we found on the street whether it would be possible to purchase a document in order to get into the U.S.," said Tom Tancredo, a congressman from Colorado. "Within about one minute, we were able to find such a person."

Immigrant smuggling rings facilitate much of the illegal traffic from Mexico. In October 2001, a Mexican news agency reported that Mexican police had arrested Joel Priego, an alleged smuggler, trying to bring seven people from India into the United States. He had charged them US$25,000 each for a voyage that had led them through Greece, Russia, Cuba, Ecuador, and Guatemala on their way to the U.S. border. Mexican officials say hundreds of bands of immigrant smugglers, known as "coyotes," operate in Mexico.

Many other routes are used to get OTMs to the U.S. border. In February 2000, the U.S. Border Patrol arrested five Sikhs in Arizona. They had left New Delhi in December and travelled to London on legitimate passports. They flew from London to Mexico City and then made their way to the border by train and other ground transport. Then they walked into the United States near Douglas, Arizona, with the help of a smuggler who kept their passports. Upon their arrest, they made refugee claims.

Mexican officials in the southern state of Chiapas detained 80,000 undocumented immigrants in 2001. Most were Central Americans, but there were also people from India, Lebanon, Iraq, and Sierra Leone. And in November 2001, a former immigration agent in Juarez, a border town, was jailed for 30 months for working for a global network that had smuggled hundreds of Iraqis and Palestinians into the United States since 1996. In December of that year, police in Matamoros arrested a man for smuggling Pakistanis, eastern Europeans, and others into the States.

Are all these people terrorists? Certainly not, but some might be. According to the German intelligence agency, 70,000 people have been trained in Osama bin Laden's school for terrorists in Afghanistan. Some want to bring jihad to the United States, and a good way to get to the United States is through Mexico. "Don't believe all terrorists come through Canada," Hector Castro, the state police commander in Matamoros, told the Associated Press in December 2001.

Steven Camarota, of the Center for Immigration Studies in Washington, D.C., says about 450,000 people are added to the illegal population of the United States every year; half come over one of the borders and the other half overstay legal entries. If the Canada-U.S. border is opened up, the 8 million unidentified people in the United States will be able to walk into Canada any time they feel like it, presenting Canada with a massive additional security risk. Clearly, the United States has work to do securing the southern part of its perimeter and tracking people who overstay their visas before Canada can feel safe about removing its border controls.

Americans, for all their recent talk about the need for secure borders, are ambivalent about the subject. The American agricultural industry, among others, has grown accustomed to the cheap labour illegal immigration provides. So have many American families who employ illegal cleaners, nannies, and gardeners. As a result, the unofficial U.S. policy has been to control illegal immigration but not to control it too much. Illegal immigration will never be eradicated, but it could be sharply curtailed if the Americans wished to invest the resources.

On a per capita basis, the American intake of immigrants is half of Canada's, even when illegal immigration is included. But that's more than 1 million immigrants a year, plenty to support a flourishing immigration industry in the United States. American universities are an important part of the equation. More than 500,000 foreign students attend American post-secondary institutions, and they are an important revenue source; most of them pay full tuition. Some "students," such as Hani Hanjour, one of the September 11 hijackers, don't show up for school after being admitted to the States on a student visa. Others do show up but forget to leave when their visas expire.

One of the terrorists in the 1993 bombing of the World Trade Center, Eyad Ismoil, had an expired student visa. That was why, in 1996, the INS proposed a new computerized system to track holders of such visas. The system would allow the U.S. government to know which visa holders hadn't enrolled or were still in the country when they shouldn't be.

The American immigration industry, led by the universities, decided the plan would be bad for business and successfully opposed it. As a result, nobody knew that Hanjour was wandering around the country preparing the September 11 assault rather than studying English at a Berlitz school in Oakland, California. If a tracking system had been in place, Hanjour might have been arrested before he could help hijack a plane. After the attacks, opponents of the plan conceded that maybe it wasn't a bad idea after all; the INS has now been mandated to set up the tracking system.

In March 2002, it became clear how much work had to be done before the INS had a functional system. That was when Rudi Dekkers, who runs a flight school in Florida, received a letter from the INS informing him that two of his students, Mohammed Atta and Marwan al-Shehhi, had been approved for student visas. Both had died by flying planes into the World Trade Center six months earlier.

American business shared the blame with the U.S. federal government for the many shortcomings of the INS. Business had been content with a system full of loopholes big enough to let in millions of people willing to work for low wages and unlikely to stand up for their rights because, as illegal immigrants, they had few.

Until September 11, such ambivalence about illegal immigration was built into the INS. Mark Reed, a former INS regional director, found that out on his first day on the job. He was rounding up illegal immigrants in San Francisco, and one day he rounded up too many. "My partner told me to pick one out and release him," Reed told the *Investor's Business Daily*. "He told me it was a common practice known as 'leaving one for seed.'"

Reed recalled that a crackdown on meat packers employing 5,000 illegal immigrants in Nebraska had been called off because of industry pressure and that, after a special operation closed the border near San Diego, funding to do the same in Texas disappeared. "The nation was not ready to stop the flow of migrant labour into the country," he said. "It wasn't that the INS didn't have a coherent immigration enforcement policy. The nation didn't want one. INS was expected to be ineffective."

Americans, justifiably, wondered why Ahmed Ressam was free to plan an attack on the Los Angeles airport after being ordered deported from Canada. But the U.S. immigration system is no model of effective enforcement. Most illegal immigrants caught by INS officers are not sent home. Instead, they appeal their deportation orders, a process that can take a year or more. Most who lose the appeal disappear. Canada can't account for 28,000 people who were supposed to have been deported; the United States can't account for 300,000.

This lackadaisical approach was not confined to American officials based in the United States. Michael Springmann, a consular official in Saudi Arabia from 1987 to 1989, told the *St. Petersburg (Florida) Times* that, under pressure from his bosses in the State Department, he issued more than 100 visas to unqualified applicants. "Keep the Saudis happy," he said he was told.

The Americans have long had a policy of keeping the oil-rich Saudis happy, ignoring the Saudis' involvement in the Islamist extremism that led to the atrocities of September 11. Al-Qaeda and the Taliban got their ideas from the Wahhabi sect of Islam, which dominates Saudi Arabia. The Saudi government permitted the recruitment of 25,000 young Saudis to wage jihad against the West, yet the indulgent American attitude was still in place in 2001 when 15 of the 19 hijackers' visas were granted in Saudi Arabia. Three of the hijackers did not even have to meet U.S. officials to get their visas. They picked them up at travel agencies in Saudi Arabia, using a U.S. program called Visa Express.

Hanjour was the only hijacker with a student visa. The others had B-1 or B-2 visas, issued with minimal scrutiny to business people and tourists. A total of 7.1 million visas of various kinds were issued by the United States in 2001. Another 17 million visitors, including people implicated in terrorism, were citizens of countries for which the United States does not require visas, such as Britain, France, and Canada. Many of these visitors overstay. The chances of being picked up by one of the 2,000 enforcement officers employed by the INS (as of the end of 2001) are slim.

The Americans also questioned why it was so easy for Ressam to obtain a valid Canadian passport in the name of Benni Noris. Good question. But Canada, should it contemplate removing its customs and immigration officials from the U.S. border, will want to be assured that it is no longer child's play for terrorists and other criminals to obtain identity documents in the United States. Several hijackers had driver's licences from Virginia, though none lived in that state. Most states required that applicants show a lease or some other document proving they actually lived there; Virginia required only a notarized affidavit. Small-time crooks, in exchange for a few hundred dollars, were happy to sign the forms swearing the hijackers were residents. Virginia driver's licences could be used to obtain other documents, allowing people to legitimize themselves. Illegal immigrants had been streaming into Virginia for years to avail themselves of this service before it was hastily ended on September 21, 2001.

The United States, like Canada, does not have a national identity card. The driver's licence serves that function. And Virginia was not the only state where it was absurdly easy to obtain one. Some states knowingly issued licences to illegal immigrants. In the United States, fake driver's licences good enough to get you on a plane can be bought for as little as $50. Residency forms and bank records can also be bought; so can U.S. social security cards, which all 19 hijackers had. The September 11 terrorists had all the identification they would have needed to be waved through the Canadian border.

Canada and the United States are parts of a global village in which, at any moment, millions of people are moving from one country to another, and in which billions of dollars' worth of goods move across borders every day. In such a world, porous borders were seen to be good because they facilitated commerce. After September 11, porous borders were seen to be bad because they facilitated the murderous schemes of terrorists.

Suddenly examples of our vulnerability to unwanted intrusion were everywhere. In October 2001, Italian authorities discovered Amir Farid Rizk, an Egyptian-born Canadian citizen, in a container that had left Port Said, Egypt, for Toronto. The container had been turned into a living space for its occupant, who had a bed and toilet, a laptop computer, two cell phones, and several identity documents, including a Canadian passport. If he hadn't been discovered in Italy, he wouldn't have had much trouble at his destination, since Canadian authorities rarely inspect arriving containers.

Of course, he probably wouldn't have been discovered at a U.S. port, either. Millions of containers arrive at U.S. ports each year, and before September 11 only 2 percent of them were inspected. If terrorists wanted to smuggle nuclear, chemical, or biological weapons into the United States, a container would be as good a way as a pre-cleared truck from Canada.

U.S. port authorities have X-ray machines to see inside containers but they don't have enough of them, or enough people, to inspect every one of the 7.8 million sealed containers carrying US$480 billion worth of goods that arrived in 2000. What they can do is inspect a higher proportion, so that potential enemies know the risk of apprehension is, at least, greater than negligible.

Total control of the ports or the borders is not only impossible, it is undesirable, because if it were ever attained, North Americans would no longer enjoy a free and open society. But it would be wrong to consider all measures to upgrade security as infringements on liberty. Both the United States and Canada are installing better systems for identifying and tracking visitors. Biometric identity cards, integrated databases, and enhanced information sharing are part of this process. These will not eliminate the threat of terrorist attacks but they will reduce it, thereby enhancing freedom for everybody but terrorists.

Few would argue that all immigration should be stopped, or that North America should no longer be a haven for refugees. Nor would many people wish to close the continent off to the millions of visitors and temporary workers who spend time in North America every year. The issue is not whether people should be able to come here from other parts of the world, but whether they should have the right to violate residency rules and to falsify their identities. They do not have such rights; Canada and the United States have every reason to take whatever measures are necessary to prevent them from doing these things.

The growth of mass travel and mass immigration has outpaced the abilities of governments to keep track of who is present on their territories. Yet not only do governments have a right to this information, they have an obligation to obtain it to protect their citizens from harm. The Canadian government has been particularly negligent. As mentioned, it made no move, until after September 11, to replace the easily forged IMM 1000 landed immigrant identity document. And it has always been more keen to deliver Canadian passports quickly than to ensure they get into the right hands. Only after the attacks did the government announce plans to expand back-ground checks on passport applicants and to make the passport booklet more secure.

Knowing who's in the country means knowing not only who has come in but who has left. The U.S. government plans to introduce, by 2004, a system to track non-citizens entering and leaving the country, a group that, in 2000, numbered 350 million people. Canada, which has no plans for a similar system of its own, has asked the Americans to exclude Canadians from the new system. This is likely to become a highly sensi-tive, contentious issue. In the absence of major reforms to Canada's immigration and refugee system, excluding Canada from the entry-exit program would be like building concrete walls on three sides of a building and leaving balsa wood and open windows on the fourth side. Small wonder that INS offi-cials, speaking anonymously, told United Press International that the new system will eventually apply to Canadians whether Canada likes it or not.

In 1985, when the Supreme Court of Canada stated, in the *Singh* decision, that all refugee claimants have a right to an oral hearing, it seemed reasonable enough. But the court's ruling has been interpreted by the government and lower courts to mean that even the most transparently fraudulent arrivals have the right not only to a hearing but to multiple appeals of nega-tive decisions. The process can take years, during which the claimants collect welfare and enjoy other social benefits.

In no other country does the government so severely con-strain its ability to carry out one of its primary duties: to protect its citizens by denying entry to unidentified people. Canada is the only independent country that does not confidently assert its right to control its own territory. The *Singh* decision, as it's been interpreted, is extremely damaging to Canada; a govern-ment attentive to the national interest could invoke the notwithstanding clause of the Charter of Rights to nullify it.

Even within the confines of the *Singh* decision, the government could reduce the numbers of false refugee claimants by establishing a competent tribunal, detaining undocumented arrivals, reducing the layers of appeal, and swiftly deporting failed claimants.

It chooses not to do so, preferring to take its direction from the immigration and refugee industry. In pandering to that industry, the Canadian government has inflicted far greater damage to Canadian sovereignty than any American demands have done.

James Bissett, former head of the Canadian immigration service, is highly knowledgeable on the subject. After leaving the civil service in 1992, he spent five years in Russia helping the government there set up a new immigration department. He's in regular contact with international experts on refugee and migration issues and sees the Americans' push for a secure North American perimeter not as a threat to Canada's sovereignty but as something that could bolster it.

"I think it's the only hope we have of getting a sensible asylum system," he says. "Otherwise this government is not going to admit it made a mistake. It never has in the past; it's not going to now." And when the United States implements exit controls, he says, Canada probably will be forced to do the same. "I think the spinoff of September 11 is that it will force Canadians to realize that immigration is important and that it shouldn't be left to lawyers, special interest groups, and politicians who only care about one thing: keeping their party in power."

CHAPTER FOUR

THE HIJACKING OF IMMIGRATION

BACK IN 1976, PETER STOLLERY, THE LIBERAL MEMBER OF Parliament for Toronto-Spadina, was angry. The immigration program was not bringing in the voters the Liberals needed to refresh their ranks of loyal supporters. Stollery decided to give the newly appointed immigration minister, Bud Cullen, a piece of his mind. He wrote Cullen a letter that included the following:

> Before you get completely overwhelmed by the officials in your Immigration Department, I would like to bring to your attention the fact that immigration has, for all practical purposes, become useless to us as Liberals as a political weapon. I think this is serious. Immigration is a contributory factor to the winning of many constituencies in Canada, not only my own constituency of Spadina in Toronto, but also in Trinity, Davenport, The Yorks, Peel-Dufferin-Simcoe and Mississauga. I know it is an

important factor in some of the Montreal constituencies and Vancouver. I cannot understand why we have allowed such an important matter to be treated in such a bureaucratic fashion without political consideration. It is the kind of thing that has led to our decline in the country. The Prime Minister has remarked about our loss of support in the ethnic communities, but the one ready weapon we have – immigration – we turn over to the bureaucrats 100%.

I don't like to flay a dead horse, but our stupid decision not to admit any Portuguese-Angolans and to make it effectively impossible for most nominated ones to come from the bastion Liberal area of Portugal – the Azores – has practically lost us the Portuguese community. If we don't make a comeback and make it fast, we can forget about it. The Portuguese are in the same position as the Italians were twenty years ago. It is a new community interested in expanding through bringing friends and relatives to our country. We allowed the Italian community to expand and guaranteed them as Liberal communities for many years. The Portuguese community . . . is being thrown away. As a politician who likes politics and who does not want to see a disintegration of the Liberal Party in this country the way it has disintegrated elsewhere, this makes me very angry.

The "nominated" immigrants to whom Stollery referred were a class of immigrants known as "nominated relatives" who were assessed under the points system as independent immigrants but got extra credits for being related to someone already in Canada. In the letter, Stollery went on to describe the cases of Portuguese families who came to Canada while their sons were doing military service. By the time the sons got out of the military, they were too old to be sponsored by their parents. Yet they didn't have the education or skills to qualify for admission, even as nominated relatives. Stollery continued:

> Do your officials not realize that in the Azores the schooling only went to Grade 3 until very recently? You must realize that 66% of all our immigrants from Portugal come from the Azores and they are practically 100% Liberal. The other 33% of immigrants coming from Portugal come mostly from Northern Portugal which is the bastion of Conservative Portugal . . . In the Portuguese cases the parents are so confused because they have supported the government, have supported the Prime Minister when times were tough, as they are now, and yet we do nothing for them in return. But, we had better smarten up or it won't matter.

This letter is as revealing today as it was when it was written a quarter-century ago. It encapsulates the ongoing struggle over immigration policy, a struggle between those who think it should serve the interests of Canada and those who think it should serve the interests of the party in power. It tells us how politicians talk about immigration policy in private. Stollery was unusual only insofar as he committed everyday backroom talk to paper. Although many might find his letter offensive, it certainly did no harm to his career. In 1981, Prime Minister Pierre Trudeau rewarded him for loyal service to the party by installing him in the Senate.

Who gets in? No country – not even Canada, with the most expansive immigration policy in the world – can let everybody in. Access to Canada must be rationed. Immigration policy is about deciding who gets those precious ration tickets. Should the people admitted be the ones most likely to do well in Canada or the ones most likely to vote for the government that admitted them?

At times, the national interest was ascendant. It was a Liberal government, under Lester Pearson, that invented the points system in 1967. The idea was that, since Canada could admit only a limited number of immigrants, it might as well select those with the best chance of succeeding. This implied a preference for people who could speak English or French and had occupational skills that were in demand. International experts on immigration applauded the points system. Australia liked it so much that it copied it. Critics of U.S. policy bewailed the fact that the Americans didn't have it, which was why, the critics said, immigrants to the United States didn't do as well as immigrants to Canada.

But Liberals like Stollery have been fighting against the points system since the day it was enacted, because it is a lousy way to harvest voters. The independent immigrants selected under the points system don't need to be sponsored, so they may be of any nationality, including ones that have not established large communities in Canada. If they are not part of a large community, they are harder to organize on behalf of the Liberal cause.

Because they are educated, they are less malleable, less likely to be the obedient Liberals that politicians expect the program to deliver. These independent immigrants may see no reason why they should vote for the party that happened to be in office when they arrived, should the policies and performance of that party not meet their expectations.

You don't guarantee your political future by letting in immigrants like that. What you want, if you're a Liberal, is large communities of people of the same nationality. Politicians love chain immigration, whereby someone sponsors his parents, who then sponsor other offspring, who then sponsor fiancés, who then sponsor their parents, and so on. In this way, geographically concentrated ethnic communities are established and enlarged. Organizations are formed to represent these communities, and the politicians are ultra-solicitous of the views of the leaders of these organizations because the leaders tell their members how they are expected to vote.

To a Peter Stollery, it does not matter that the 25-year-old ex-soldier with grade 3 education is illiterate not only in English but in his native language as well. The only writing he ever has to do, as far as the politician is concerned, is to put an X next to the Liberal candidate's name every four years or so on the election ballot.

From his perch in the Senate, Peter Stollery can observe with satisfaction the triumph of his views. Huge numbers of immigrants are brought to Canada for no apparent reason except to bolster existing ethnic communities. And the Immigration and Refugee Board is perpetuated, despite expert advice that it be replaced, because it provides lucrative jobs for party supporters.

This attitude is deeply ingrained in the Liberal Party. "It goes back 45 years," says Jack Manion, who worked in the department when Jack Pickersgill was minister in the mid-1950s. "Pickersgill established the Citizenship Liaison Branch," Manion, now retired, recalled at his Ottawa home, "with a mandate to promote closer connections with the various ethnic groups. The people appointed were Liberals. For example, the citizenship liaison officer in Toronto was Andy Thompson, who later became leader of the Ontario Liberal Party and a senator. Andy made no secret of the fact that he was promoting the Liberal Party to the ethnic community.

"I think the Liberals are so deeply involved with the ethnic community, so beholden to it, that it is difficult for them to do anything other than what they have done. They exacerbate this by appointing a minister" – he was speaking of former immigration minister Elinor Caplan – "who comes from a heavily ethnic area and has been associated with ethnic politics for her whole adult life."

Cullen, the minister Stollery was trying to influence in

1976, had followed Robert Andras, a rarity in the portfolio in that he had a national-interest view of immigration. Andras, from Thunder Bay, was not a captive of Toronto ethnic communities as were such Chrétien-era ministers as Sergio Marchi and Caplan. Whereas Chrétien's ministers were committed to a more-is-better approach, Andras thought attention had to be paid to the possible negative impacts of too much immigration on the urban environment. He argued against rapid population growth.

The 1970s and the first half of the 1980s are remembered by those still in government as an exciting time to work in immigration; it was a time when what was best for the country was the basis of decision-making. In a 1974–75 policy review, all government departments were asked to choose net (immigration minus emigration) levels of 50,000 to 100,000 or 100,000 to 200,000. "The vast majority of departments said the lower level is preferable," recalled a senior official now in another branch of government. "Experts were doing analysis, and the analysis was saying lower immigration was more manageable and had less environmental impact. In the 1970s, the issue had not yet become politicized."

Still, it was under Andras that the clientele began its capture of the immigration program. Andras enunciated three goals: family reunification, refugee protection, and economic development. The problem is that the third goal conflicts with the first two: immigrants selected for their skills outperform the host population economically, but immigrants related to someone in Canada or who make refugee claims tend to underperform the existing population.

If a program is predicated on national interest, the largest group of immigrants should be independents selected for their skills and education. Under changes to the Immigration Act introduced in 1976 and proclaimed in 1978, that goal became harder to achieve because, in response to the demands of immigrant communities, the government eased regulations for admitting family members. As a result, the proportion of sponsored (family-class) immigrants rose and that of independent (skilled) immigrants fell.

The most important change was little noticed; its significance is still poorly understood. Previously, parents had to be 60 years old before they could come to Canada as sponsored immigrants. By the new rules, a parent of any age could come. Opening the gates to working-age parents opened the gates to extended families from Third World countries.

The parent of a 20-year-old immigrant from a wealthy country such as France or Japan has little reason to follow his offspring to Canada and will almost never do so. Such a parent will probably be in his 40s or 50s and at the peak of his working career. A 40-year-old parent living in a poor country, on the other hand, often upgrades his economic status by coming to Canada, which has social benefits far exceeding those available at home.

Such a parent, once here, could now sponsor dependent children. For the first time, the brothers and sisters of the original immigrant could come to Canada without the scrutiny of the points system. For some of these parents, landed immigrant status is in itself an income-producing asset: the parents can go back to their homeland and negotiate marriages for their offspring on the understanding that the fiancé's family will eventually also be able to come, thanks to Canada's family reunification rules.

Alan Green of Queen's University and David Green of the University of British Columbia, economists who have analyzed the Canadian program, point out that shifts in the composition of the intake create winners and losers. Reducing the proportion of skilled immigrants and increasing that of unskilled and less-skilled ones – as happens when relatives and refugees are favoured – lowers the wages of Canadians who compete with the newly arrived workers. Unskilled workers lose, and employers of unskilled workers win. But employers who need educated people adept in English lose because the program accepts fewer of them. Ethnic communities wanting to expand and refugee activists also win as the emphasis shifts away from independents.

Still, the Stollery philosophy of manipulating immigration for partisan purposes had not yet been fully embraced by the start of the 1980s, as was evident from the way immigration levels were managed during Pierre Trudeau's tenure as prime minister. When immigration is managed according to national interest, the numbers coming in are adjusted depending on economic cycles. An economy in recession cannot absorb a surge of new workers, so a well-run immigration program will reduce its intake during a downturn. When business is booming and jobs are plentiful, the tap can be reopened.

This practice was followed in the Trudeau era. As a result, immigration fell between 1974 and 1978, rebounded from 1978 to 1980, and dropped again during the first half of the 1980s. By 1985, after the end of Trudeau's term, total immigration had dropped to 84,000, well below the post–World War II average of 150,000. Such cautious, thoughtful management gives priority to the needs of the country and the welfare of the existing workforce. But it does little to augment the ranks of party supporters, and it is anathema to the lawyers, consultants, and service agencies that live off the program and need a steady supply of new customers.

Ironically, though the Liberals pride themselves on being Canada's immigration party, it wasn't until the Conservative government of Brian Mulroney took office in 1984 that the notion of using immigration for partisan purposes gained almost total ascendancy. The Tories instigated a massive increase in immigration levels. The total of 84,000 immigrants in Mulroney's first year in power had climbed to 256,000 by 1993, Mulroney's last year. Mulroney's most dramatic departure was to make these high levels permanent. His was the first government in Canadian history to increase, rather than decrease, immigration during a recession. Predictably, this exacerbated unemployment and made life even more difficult for the lower-income Canadians competing with the new labour market entrants for a dwindling number of jobs.

Why did the Tories do it? The immigration department had expressed concern about declining fertility among Canadian women, which would result in an aging population and eventual population decline. Perhaps Mulroney's government believed that a massive influx of newcomers was needed to counterbalance this trend (even though the government's own demographic review demonstrated that immigration can neither alleviate population aging nor, except at politically impossible levels, provide continual population growth). More likely, the Tories, emboldened by their electoral sweep, thought it was time they harvested some new voters of their own. Permanent high levels were also what the immigration industry wanted. The new policy satisfied both the communities and the industry, while feeding Tory fantasies of supplanting the Liberals as the preferred party of ethnic Canada.

It is natural enough that immigrants want to bring members of their extended families to Canada. They have every right to lobby governments to comply with their wishes. It is also natural for a government to refuse such demands if it deems them not in the national interest. That's what happens in Australia, another Commonwealth country with a large foreign-born population and a strong tradition of multi-ethnic immigration. Australia's political leaders have no problem saying no to the ethnic communities; Canada's leaders don't dare.

The Tories continued what the Liberals had started by making more concessions to demands to broaden the family class. A new word entered the language of the policy-makers: "stakeholders." These included ethnic communities, non-governmental organizations feeding off the immigration program, and a growing army of lawyers and consultants. Tory immigration ministers had no apparent interest in the question "What's best for the country?" The important question was: "What do the stakeholders want?"

The stakeholders wanted to be able to bring in not just children under 19 but adult offspring as well. And the Tory government acquiesced. The result was that a major new flow of non-selected, and so mostly uneducated and unskilled, immigrants began arriving. The disconnect between the announced economic goal of Canada – to build a high-tech, knowledge-based economy – and an immigration program tilting ever more towards newcomers unequipped to participate in such an economy was now complete. The Tories had turned Canada's immigration program over to the stakeholders whose political support they coveted.

The next step was to turn the refugee program over to the stakeholders as well. The Supreme Court's *Singh* decision in 1985 gave them an opportunity to do just that. The *Singh* decision stated that the Canadian Charter of Rights and Freedoms gave refugee claimants the right to an oral hearing. Previously, refugee claims had been decided by the Refugee Status Advisory Committee, which reviewed a transcript of an interview conducted by an immigration officer. The Supreme Court decision could have been implemented in ways that left Canada with a credible refugee system similar to those of other Western countries. An official at the border or airport could have conducted hearings to eliminate obviously frivolous claims, such as those from citizens of democratic countries. The more serious claims could have been referred to a tribunal staffed by judges chosen for their experience, expertise, and impartiality.

Instead, the Tory government created the Immigration and Refugee Board and staffed it with amateurs chosen from refugee advocacy groups and the ranks of Tory party workers. A refugee system that had won a United Nations award for excellence became an international laughingstock. Canada's acceptance rate for refugee claimants before the creation of the IRB had been around 20 percent, generous by international standards. (Most countries approve 15 percent or fewer of refugee claims for the simple reason that most are unfounded.) The Tories' IRB, after its establishment in 1988, approved 90 percent or more of the refugee claims before it.

The arrival of the IRB was a godsend for the smuggling gangs, who began sending thousands of clients to Canada. Some of these clients, before the creation of the IRB, would have applied to come under the immigration program, but the IRB seemed a better choice for many. Applicants for admission under the immigration program often have to wait years for approval. Thanks to the IRB, a prospective immigrant could circumvent the system simply by reciting a standard story of "persecution," thereby gaining entry immediately. And there was another key advantage to coming through the IRB: refugees are eligible for welfare, sponsored immigrants are not.

The IRB's acceptance rates are lower under the Liberals than they were under the Tories but are still absurd by international standards. Because of them, Canada does not really have a refugee determination system. Instead, the IRB runs a parallel immigration program in which self-selected immigrants are accepted as refugees, although most would not be so defined anywhere else in the world.

The creation of the IRB by Mulroney's government is inexplicable except as an attempt to curry favour with the "stakeholders." But the Tories were wrong if they thought most foreign-born Canadians wanted to see their adopted country make a fool of itself on the world stage by accepting tens of thousands of bogus refugees. Most immigrants played by the rules to come to Canada, waiting patiently until their applications were accepted. Such people are unsympathetic to other immigrants whom they regard as queue-jumpers. Chinese and other foreign-language papers in Canada have often been scathing in their attacks on the refugee system.

By attracting an ever-increasing flow of refugee claimants, the IRB created a major new legal industry dependent on public funds. Legal aid for refugees amounted to more than $21 million in 2000. These lawyers, many of whom are active in refugee advocacy groups as well, are fierce lobbyists for the current system. They too are "stakeholders" and are treated with deference by immigration ministers.

The triumph of the stakeholders resulted in more relatives and more refugee claimants. Something had to give, and that was independent immigration. In 1971, 32 percent of immigrants were assessed by the points system. By 1994, skilled immigrants had dwindled to a mere 13 percent of the total intake. The rest were immediate families accompanying independent immigrants, relatives sponsored later, and refugees.

As of 2001, the independent group had rebounded to 23 percent, still well below where it had been 30 years earlier. To camouflage the fact that so few immigrants were being selected on the basis of skills, the immigration department in recent years began including accompanying spouses and children of selected immigrants in the independent category. Even normally reliable Statistics Canada publications misleadingly show a majority of independent immigrants. The important number, of course, is the percentage of people actually assessed for education, language, and occupational skills. And, at 23 percent, it's a small part of the intake.

Even immigration composed entirely of highly skilled English- and French-speaking people would not necessarily be of great benefit to those already living in Canada. Immigration has little or no impact on per capita incomes, since almost all the additional wealth produced by the newcomers winds up where it belongs: in the pockets of the immigrants who produced it. But the presence of skilled immigrants is helpful even if the benefits are not easily quantified. They work in the kinds of knowledge industries that an advanced economy needs to encourage, facilitating the growth of these industries. And they augment the public treasury rather than drain it, because they pay more in taxes than they claim in public benefits.

Not everyone chosen through the points system succeeds in Canada. But since entry tickets have to be rationed in some way, it's in the country's interest to maximize the number that go to those most likely to succeed. Someone whose occupation is in demand, who has a good education, and who speaks one of Canada's official languages has a better chance of success than someone lacking such qualifications.

As of May 2002, independent immigrants were required to score a minimum 70 points, allotted on the basis of age, education, occupation, language ability, and experience. People aged 21 to 44 get the maximum 10 points for age; those over 48 get none. Occupations are assigned points according to demand. Physiotherapists and cooks receive the maximum 10 while occupations not in demand, such as barbers and biologists, receive the minimum 1 point. The biologist would still have a better chance of entry than the barber, because he gets 17 points for education and training versus only 2 for the barber.

Those who bypass the points system and come as sponsored family members don't do very well. In a report to Parliament in 1990, the economist Don DeVoretz sounded a warning about the shift from selected to self-selected immigration. Whereas previous waves of Third World immigrants, because they were selected, caught up to Canadian-born people in income, the post-1978 group was not catching up and, said DeVoretz, "may never equal earlier immigrant income performance."

These are Peter Stollery's Liberal voters with grade 3 education. Most are undoubtedly good, hard-working people, the sort who would have prospered in Canada in the early 1950s when there were still opportunities for uneducated people. In the 21st century, when mechanics and miners are expected to be both literate and numerate, there are fewer opportunities.

The result? Immigrants arriving since the 1976 changes

were put into effect in 1978 have fallen 40 percent below the income levels of both earlier immigrants and Canadian-born citizens. Family-class immigrants are the only ones whose use of welfare grows higher the longer they stay in Canada. Family-class immigrants are not even supposed to go on welfare; their sponsors guarantee as much for 10 years after their arrival. Yet a study published by the immigration department in 1996 found that only three years after their arrival in Canada, 20 percent of sponsored parents and grandparents were using welfare, twice the rate of tax filers overall. In 2001 the Ontario government paid $100 million in social assistance to immigrants whose sponsoring relatives had defaulted on their obligations.

Ottawa doesn't pursue deadbeat sponsors, nor does it require them to post a bond. Such measures would amount to admitting that there are costs associated with immigration, and that admission would fly in the face of accepted ideology. The government's solution to the problem of sponsorship breakdown? Legislation, passed in 2001, that lowered from ten years to three the period during which a sponsor has to assume responsibility for a spouse or same-sex partner. Meanwhile, we allow immigrants on welfare to sponsor relatives, virtually guaranteeing that they, too, will wind up on welfare.

The Liberal government does not care if immigrants go on welfare, or if sponsors ignore their legal obligations. All that matters is that the stakeholders – the people who benefit from immigration – are happy. The government alters rules and policies to appease this lobby, and the lobby is expected to reward the party with its support.

Jack Manion estimates the costs of the immigration program at $4 billion a year. These costs – which include welfare for refugees and sponsored immigrants, legal aid for refugee claimants, health and dental care, IRB hearings, deportation of criminals and failed refugees, English-language training, and other services – are borne by taxpayers. But taxpayers are never heard from on the issue because they are not organized. Their contrary views on immigration and refugee matters, as expressed through public opinion polling, are considered irrelevant.

This used to be called pork-barrel politics; the more polite term, used by political scientists, is clientelism. It's not confined to immigration, of course; many government programs have clienteles that profit from them. Occasionally the system back-fires, as when an auditor in 2000 found widespread waste and abuse in the administration of millions of dollars of grants by the human resources department. There's a flurry in the press and in Parliament, but it dies down and the issue goes away. The important thing is that the clients, in that case the grant recipients, were happy.

By the end of the Mulroney years, the Tories had ceded power to the stakeholders over most of the immigration and refugee program. They had, however, retained one important lever: they could lower annual immigration levels should it be deemed necessary. During the brief reign of Prime Minister Kim Campbell, a poll of senior bureaucrats indicated that all but one thought the annual intake should come down by at least 20,000. But the 1993 election intervened, Campbell and the Tories were crushed, and the new Liberal government had other ideas.

The Liberals had offered voters a Red Book of campaign promises, one of which was to increase immigration to a level of 1 percent of the total population. This is an enormous level that seemed to be based on the quaint yet oft-heard notion that "Canada is a big country with lots of wide-open spaces, so we can take lots of new people." The fact is that modern immigrants are urban people with little interest in wide-open spaces. Forty percent of them go to the Greater Toronto Area, 20 percent to Vancouver, and almost all the rest to Montreal and a few other cities. Under the 1 percent policy, Canada would accept almost a million new people every three years into an existing urban population of about 10 million. This would fire up the real estate and immigration industries but would be of no benefit to anyone else.

Canada is the only country in which a proposal to raise immigration to 1 percent of the population would be taken seriously, let alone pledged by the major political party. That level in the United States would almost triple immigration there, to 2.9 million a year. No other country contemplates taking such a step. As yet, the Liberals have not implemented it. But the 1 percent policy marked the end of any serious planning in which the numbers could be adjusted to reflect economic conditions, such as high unemployment rates, or demographic change, such as the entry of the echo generation – the children of the baby boomers – into the labour market. No debate about levels takes place in the immigration department. All the minister can do is instruct his officials to edge the annual intake ever closer to 1 percent of population, in good times and bad.

Anyone who suggests that levels ought to be lowered is, predictably, attacked as being anti-immigrant. This charge and worse was levelled at Preston Manning, then leader of the Reform Party, when he suggested in 1992 that levels ought to be brought back to the post-war norm of 150,000 a year. Yet 150,000 newcomers are 62,000 more than Pierre Trudeau's government admitted in its last year in power, and Trudeau was never called anti-immigrant.

"It's one of the great tragedies of immigration policy-making in Canada that it has become so politicized," says a senior bureaucrat. "When you try to argue that a lower level might be better, you're accused of having ulterior motives based on racism or some other anti-immigrant sentiment. We've lost the capacity to have a debate."

The economists Alan Green and David Green, in their historical survey of the economic goals of Canada's immigration policy, seemed almost at a loss to explain how it had arrived at its current peculiar state. "The current policy appears to have been set by 'true believers' who hold firmly to a faith in the long term benefits of high levels of immigration," they concluded. "The trouble with this is that the government has not presented evidence to justify this faith."

"True believers" is an apt description of those in the immigration department in 2002. No one is allowed to mention costs or negative consequences. On the rare occasions when a proposal slips through without the stakeholders' approval, retribution is swift. In 2001, the department suggested upgrading educational requirements for skilled immigrants. In response, the stakeholders told MPs in ethnic ridings to attack, and the government quickly backpedalled.

Stakeholders seem to believe that Canada should not have the right to require anything of immigrants, either qualifications before they get here or obligations once they have arrived. Immigrants already in Canada should be able to sponsor anyone they want. After all, goes the reasoning, immigration is a source of prosperity, and Canada would be in dire straits with less of it. It's taken for granted that we must continue increasing levels to avoid becoming a nation of seniors.

This nonsense reached its full expression in the regime of Elinor Caplan, the minister who produced the new immigration bill that became law late in 2001. The stakeholders wanted further liberalization of sponsorship rules, and Caplan responded by reducing from 19 to 18 the age at which a relative could be sponsored. She increased from 19 to 21 the age at which a dependent child could be sponsored by a parent. In many countries, it is easy enough to buy a birth certificate that reduces one's age. The result is that people can now sponsor adult offspring as old, in some cases, as 30. Caplan also removed restrictions on the sponsoring of newcomers who were likely to make excessive demands on the health care system.

All these measures were hostile to the national interest. As we've seen, expanding family-class immigration accentuates the decline in economic performance of new immigrants. Caplan's bill guarantees that Canada will have ever more people competing for ever fewer jobs that do not require language or other skills. And it means more immigrants on welfare. All that mattered to the government – now as in 1976, when Stollery wrote to Cullen – was the support of the sponsors, and the prospect of unskilled newcomers voting Liberal.

All the more puzzling, then, that after shepherding this shameful legislation through Parliament, Caplan was demoted to a lesser portfolio in January 2002. Had she not done exactly what the Liberal Party expected of her? By the time she was bumped to the revenue department, the hijacking of the immigration program by its clientele was complete.

CHAPTER FIVE

CREATION OF A MYTHOLOGY

In the winter of 2001, the University of Toronto offered a course through its School of Continuing Studies on the subject of immigration in Canada. The course description stated: "Canada needs immigrants to sustain our economic growth and compensate for our declining birth rate. A massive inflow of young immigrants in the workforce is required to support the needs of retired baby boomers – about 500,000 [a year] over the next 20 years, more than twice the current rate."

These statements have no connection to reality. Economic growth, in Canada or elsewhere, does not depend on immigration. Nor does Canada need, now or in future, a massive influx of young immigrants to support retired baby boomers, none of whom will reach age 65 until 2012.

That course description summarizes in one crisp paragraph the mythology of immigration in Canada. This mythology is built on two false beliefs: that the economic prosperity and the demographic survival of Canada both depend on immigration. These assumptions are widely accepted because they are

94

regularly repeated by politicians and others with a stake in maintaining and expanding Canada's immigration program.

The mythology is powerful because it is rooted in fear: fear that lack of population growth will create poverty, fear that an aging society will not be able to support its retired people, fear that necessary tasks will go undone for want of people to do them. Only when we see that these fears are unfounded can rational discussion about immigration policy become possible.

THE DEMOGRAPHIC MYTH

"Canada's population growth is negative, so we need immigration to maintain a certain population for our own good." The speaker, an intelligent and experienced Vancouver judge, offered this information to me as if it were common knowledge, something every informed person knows. He was incredulous when told that there are more births than deaths each year in Canada and that our population, therefore, would increase even without any immigration at all.

One part of the judge's statement was at least partly correct: "We need immigration to maintain a certain population." While we don't need immigration now to maintain our population, we will eventually. The population replacement rate is 2.1 babies per woman. When women have, on average, 2.1 children each, one generation replaces another without any immigration. (The extra one-tenth of a child is needed to compensate for childhood deaths and childless couples.) Canada's fertility rate in 2001 was 1.5, well below replacement. Assuming fertility does not rebound, the Canadian population, in the absence of immigration, eventually will decline.

The common belief, perpetuated by the exaggerations of people promoting higher immigration levels, is that decline is already happening and that the need for immigration is urgent. Despite below-replacement fertility, however, Canadian women are still having enough children to keep the population growing, without immigration, until 2015.

Why doesn't the population decline immediately if fertility is below replacement? Assume a couple in their 20s decide to have only one child. That decision will ultimately result in a one-person drop in the Canadian population. But it won't happen until about 60 years in the future, when both parents of the only child are dead.

Every five years, Statistics Canada takes a census of the Canadian population. When the results of the 2001 census were announced in March 2002, they showed that the population had grown by only 4 percent since the 1996 census, matching the lowest five-year growth rate the country had ever experienced. Coverage of this information in the major newspapers bordered on hysterical. Taken for granted in all of it was the idea that the absence of population growth, or even a slower rate of population growth, inevitably leads to disaster.

Andrew Coyne, a columnist in the *National Post*, had a way to avoid this supposedly looming disaster. Canada, he proposed in a front-page article, should increase annual immigration to 850,000 a year with a goal of creating a population of 215 million by the end of the century. The article, which some readers may understandably have viewed as an attempt at satire, was intended to be taken seriously. Coyne positions himself on the far right of the political spectrum, and the political right has good reasons to like unrestricted immigration.

In a *Globe and Mail* interview, meanwhile, David Baxter, an economist who claims to be an expert in demographics, said that the new census proves Canada must increase its immigration every year to avoid the unspeakable: a population that stops growing. A few years earlier Baxter had done a cross-country speaking tour promoting the virtues of real estate as an investment: the real estate industry, perhaps more than any other, depends on rapid population growth for its profits. On the day the census figures were released, he called a press conference to announce that Canada's demographic situation was grim: "We're talking about a country whose population will stop growing within nine years if we don't have more immigration."

A non-growing population would be bad for the real estate industry, but there's no evidence that it would be bad for Canadians who do not work in that industry. In any case, Baxter was misinformed. According to Statistics Canada projections, if fertility stays at 1.5 and immigration remains at current levels, Canada's population will increase until about 2040, after which point, assuming those same fertility and immigration levels, it would stabilize at about 37 million.

There's a flaw in the argument that prosperity depends on population growth, a flaw so glaring that someone who has never heard of economics can see it. It's that growth can never end. Even if Canada were to achieve Andrew Coyne's vision of 215 million, it wouldn't be enough. Even if Canada were to surpass China and India as the world's most populous country, our population still could not be allowed to stop growing, not ever, lest 2 billion Canadians be plunged into poverty.

This is the cancer-cell theory of economics, a nightmare that the immigration industry and its cheerleaders insist we accept. In the mid-1980s, Mike Murphy, a demographer heading the federal government's demographic review of Canada's population future, encountered a Swedish colleague. The Swede was puzzled. "Why," he wanted to know, "are so many Canadian researchers coming to Sweden to ask how we cope with an aging population?"

Canada has a comparatively young population, younger than those of Sweden and the other industrialized countries of western Europe. Yes, Canada's birth rates have fallen. But so have those in the rest of the world, including many of the underdeveloped countries. Yes, Canada – because of declining fertility and increasing longevity – is getting older. So is the rest of the world.

Only in Canada are these trends seen as threatening. Only in Canada does the press give credence to prophets of doom such as David Baxter. Only in Canada are recommendations made that immigration be raised to 1 percent or even 2 percent of the population per year. Anywhere else such suggestions would be laughed at; in Canada, they are reported on the front pages of serious newspapers.

Every country in Europe, except Turkey, has fertility rates below the replacement level. Even Ireland, the most conservative of Catholic countries, has below-replacement fertility. Canada is the only country in which a massive increase in immigration is viewed as the necessary response to the collective decision of its people, signalled by their reproductive behaviour, that they prefer a smaller population. Canada, remember, *already* gets immigration at a per capita rate twice that of any other country. To the Europeans, we must appear unhinged.

If the doomsayers were right, the Europeans, with their aging, non-growing populations, would be in crisis. Social programs would be collapsing and the streets would be strewn with garbage for want of workers to collect it. None of this is happening. Sweden has a greater proportion of its population in the 65-and-over category than Canada has, and a lesser proportion in the 15-to-64, working-age category. How does Sweden cope? The way all countries not obsessed with the quick fix of immigration cope. By being productive. By using technology. By exporting its products rather than relying on the domestic population for market growth. By facilitating the full participation of women in the workforce. By offering excellent early childhood education programs that help children to maximize their potential.

The European countries are prospering with the same age structure Canada will have in about 20 years. Are there worker shortages? Occasionally. They're dealt with as they occur; workers are brought in from elsewhere as needed. Perhaps the European countries, if they wish to avoid population decline, may decide to increase immigration. Despite the stronger demographic case for immigration in Europe than in Canada, however, the Europeans don't make nearly as much fuss about it as Canada does.

The indisputable fact, ignored in most of the coverage of the new census data, is that Canada's population is going to stop growing. Forget the propaganda urging massive population growth. Here's what a serious writer, the biologist Edward O. Wilson, has to say on the subject.

> When the number of children per woman stays above 2.1 even slightly, the population still expands exponentially. This means that although the population climbs less and less steeply as the number approaches 2.1, humanity will still, in theory, eventually come to weigh as much as Earth and, if given enough time, will exceed the mass of the visible universe. This fantasy is a mathematician's way of saying that anything above zero population growth cannot be sustained . . . It should be obvious to anyone not in a euphoric delirium that whatever humanity does or does not do, Earth's capacity to support our species is approaching the limit.

What's happening in Europe – the advent of population stability – is going to happen in the rest of the world, Canada included. It's going to happen because the Earth cannot sustain endless population growth and because people don't want it. If they did, they would have three, four, and five children instead of none, one, or two. Even if Canadians wanted to turn Andrew Coyne's delirium into reality, they couldn't because the rest of the world, with its falling birth rates, can't supply us with hundreds of millions of immigrants.

So the real issue is: At what level do we want population growth to stop? To answer this question, we first need to understand this demographic principle: any combination of constant below-replacement fertility with a constant immigration level eventually results in population stability. This principle tells us that below-replacement fertility is an extremely powerful phenomenon. No government that wants to survive can raise immigration levels high enough to sustain population growth in the face of a fertility rate of 1.5. Even a colossal intake – say, 600,000 newcomers a year – combined with the current fertility rate of 1.5 eventually will produce a stable population of 50 million Canadians. (The population would rise above 50 million before falling back and stabilizing at that level.)

Immigration of 600,000 a year would be unmanageable and, from a national security standpoint, intolerable. To almost every Canadian it would be unacceptable. For those reasons, it is not going to happen. Barring a dramatic rebound in fertility, therefore, Canada's population will stabilize somewhere well below 50 million.

When we ask how large we want Canada's stable population to be, we're really asking how big we want our major cities to be, since virtually all immigrants settle in major cities. Three-quarters of the 7 million newcomers who will be added to an eventually stable Canadian population (should current high immigration levels prevail) will wind up in Toronto, Vancouver, and Montreal. If levels are increased, 10 million or more people may ultimately be added to the populations of these cities.

Immigration has played a major role in making Canada's cities more vibrant. Food and dining are only one obvious example. Outside Montreal, Canada 40 years ago was a gastronomic wasteland. Now, thanks largely to the culinary knowledge and skills of immigrants, Toronto, Vancouver, and many other Canadian cities boast excellent markets and restaurants offering virtually all the cuisines of the world. The contributions of immigrants have helped make Canada's biggest cities among the most liveable in the world. In fact, the liveability of our big cities is a huge asset for Canada and one that seems to be better appreciated outside Canada than within.

William M. Mercer, an international human resources consulting firm, annually ranks cities around the world for quality of life. Among the criteria used are the political and social environment, the economic situation, culture, the standards of schools and other public services, housing, recreation, and the natural environment. Significantly, the top-ranked cities on this list are small to medium-sized big cities (in the 1-to-4-million range) as opposed to megacities (10 million or more). The smaller big cities – such as Vancouver, Sydney, Stockholm, and Geneva – offer the cultural attractions, shopping, restaurants, and other agreeable features of big city life without the pollution, congestion, and higher crime rates of the megacities. That's why Paris and New York, for all their glories, ranked 31st and 41st on the 2002 ranking, while Vancouver tied for 2nd with Vienna, Toronto was 18th, and Montreal 25th. Vancouver had been 1st in 2001 but slipped because of growing congestion. If the immigration industry has its way, our three biggest cities will keep slipping down the liveability rankings.

Too much of a good thing, in other words, is a bad thing. This is a law of nature that applies to everything in life. Too much immigration will make Canada's big cities more crowded, more polluted, and more expensive – not because there is anything wrong with the immigrants who come but because that's the nature of very big cities.

Some people prefer New York–sized cities to Vancouver-sized cities. But in a vote, Canadians would choose Vancouver over New York in a landslide. The real estate industry stands to make billions of dollars from the immigration-fuelled development boom that creates urban sprawl around Canada's biggest cities, but what's in it for everyone else? Why do we want our cities permanently changed for the worse as a result of too-rapid growth fuelled by excessive immigration?

The Liberal government and its stakeholders seem to believe that immigration policy is none of the public's business. Canadians are never asked what they want. Instead, they're told that they're going to keep getting massive immigration whether they like it or not, and they're told that it's necessary.

It's all the fault of the baby boomers, or so the story goes. Too many of them were born between 1947 and 1966, 10 million to be exact, a third of the Canadian population. In 2012, the eldest boomers will reach retirement age and begin dipping into the Canada Pension Plan. Some will already have claimed early retirement benefits in 2006.

Of course, the boomers have paid billions of dollars of their earnings into the plan, but the government didn't invest all of that money the way a company or individual pension plan does. For much of its history, the Canada Pension Plan was a pay-as-you-go scheme; the payments of workers financed the pensions of the retired. This system works only when there are more workers than retirees. When the baby-boom bulge is in its retirement years, there won't be enough active workers to finance their pensions. Or so the story goes.

Making matters worse, old people aren't dying as soon as they used to. They keep living longer, exacerbating the problem. And of course old people make the greatest demands on the health care system, a system already under stress even before the boomers have had much need for it. Those with an apocalyptic view say the only solution is massive immigration, which will achieve two things. It will bring in young workers who will pay the taxes necessary to support all the retired people. And it will counteract the aging of the population and make Canada young again.

One obvious flaw in this argument is that there is no evidence yet of a worker shortage, so what justification is there for jacking up immigration levels now? Unemployment in Canada, as of May 2002, was almost 8 percent, a number that included many well-educated post-secondary graduates. Moreover, a large group of young workers have just begun entering the labour market. These are the baby-boom echo, the offspring of the boomers. They were born between 1980 and 1995 and, at 6.5 million, they are the second-largest population cohort in Canada, after the boomers themselves. A steady stream of echo boomers will be looking for their first jobs between now and

2015. Why make their entry to the labour force more difficult by bringing in armies of competing workers from abroad?

But the real flaw in the apocalyptic vision can be summed up in one word: productivity. It's why the Swedes were puzzled by the anxiety of the Canadian researchers. Didn't the Canadians know that older societies with fewer workers support themselves by becoming more productive?

Robert Brown, a professor in the Department of Statistics and Actuarial Science at the University of Waterloo, had heard what a terrible burden those aging boomers were going to be. He decided to see if the reality coincided with the doomsayers' warnings. The basic issue, he points out, is this: wealth in our society is transferred from those who work to those who do not, in the form of tax-supported programs such as education, health care, support for the unemployed, and public pensions. As a rule, transfers to the old are two and a half times as large as transfers to the young. It costs more to attend to the health of an 88-year-old than to pay for the schooling of an 8-year-old.

This looks like a dicey, worsening scenario. But when Brown ran the numbers, it became clear that productivity will come to the rescue. From 1976 to 1998, productivity increased in Canada by an average of 0.9 percent a year. Factor in the coming demographic changes with a continuation of productivity increase, and not only can we pay for the retirement of the boomers, but the retirement age, even at the height of boomer retirement in 2034, will be down to 61. If Canada's productivity increases (as it should with technological improvements), the situation becomes even rosier.

Brown is not alone in this optimistic view. Marcel Mérette, an economist at the University of Ottawa, produced a study for the Institute for Research in Public Policy in March 2002 on the economics of aging. In this study, *The Bright Side: A Positive View on the Economics of Aging*, he combined his research with an analysis of that of other economists and demographers doing advanced work in the field.

Mérette found that rising wages will help propel an increase in education and training for those in the workforce. These investments in human capital will create a burst of invention and innovation. This, in turn, will lead to technological progress, the real engine of economic growth. Historically, innovation blossoms when resources grow scarce. Just as higher energy costs triggered technological advances that increased fuel efficiency, so labour-saving technology will accompany any labour scarcity caused by population aging. Rising wages will also induce many older workers to remain in harness, further limiting labour scarcity.

Mérette points out that the investments in human capital (education and training) that accompanied aging in seven industrialized countries increased economic growth more rapidly than it would have occurred in the absence of aging. Scenarios for Canada show the same effect. Slower labour force growth is offset by higher investment in human capital and a higher participation rate. The bottom line, concludes Mérette, is counterintuitive: an aging population is actually good news, especially for the younger members of society whose incomes will rise because of it.

Besides, as the demographer Roderic Beaujot has pointed out, reduced growth in the labour force is not the same as decline. Canada is not faced with labour force decline because, unlike the European countries, it has a large immigration program. An annual intake of 200,000 a year, or 50,000 fewer immigrants than the current level, is enough to maintain a steady number of workers.

Fears for the future of the Canada Pension Plan are also unfounded. As Mérette points out, the federal government has increased funding of the CPP – that is, left money in the plan to be invested and accumulate. As a result, the plan's revenues are now greater than projected pension benefits. The CPP is solid and the boomers will collect their government pensions regardless of how many immigrants settle in Canada in future.

But, say the proponents of more immigration, won't an absence of workforce growth be a problem for a government that depends on taxpaying workers for its revenues? No, it won't. Government revenues will get a boost – just when it's needed – from taxes on the income retired people will draw from registered retirement savings plans (RRSPs) and employer-sponsored registered pension plans. Canadians already have more than $1 trillion (a sum greater than the annual gross domestic product) stashed away in these plans. And some decline can be anticipated in government spending on education and other services to the young, who will make up a smaller proportion of the population.

What does this leading-edge research do to the argument that only a huge increase in the importation of young workers can forestall a labour shortage and fiscal crisis? Destroys it utterly. Why, then, do the media focus on the disaster scenario, ignoring more credible experts who point out that the coming demographic shift isn't really worrisome? Perhaps because bad news sells more papers and wins more viewers than good news does.

What of the argument that we don't have to accept an aging society, that we can rejuvenate Canada by upping our already generous immigration intake? That too crumbles under informed analysis. The population division of the United Nations issued a report in 2000 that debunks the idea of rejuvenation through immigration. An analysis of migration flows to developed countries, it stated, provides scant evidence that immigration meaningfully reduces the age of the host population. A 1991 study done for the Organisation for Economic Co-operation and Development (OECD) analyzed the demographic consequences of migration since the end of World War II to seven countries, including Canada. Immigration, the OECD concluded, had lowered the average age in these countries by between 0.4 and 1.4 years, an insignificant number.

Immigration can't prevent population aging because recently arrived, younger immigrants make up only a small proportion of the total population. To prevent changes in the age structure, impossibly large increases in immigration would be required. For example, suppose the United States had decided in 1995 to maintain its ratio of 5.2 persons aged 15 to 64 for every one person 65 or older. To achieve this, the UN study found, the United States would have had to bring in 593 million immigrants between 1995 and 2050, an annual intake more than 10 times the current level. Under this scheme, by 2050 the United States would have a population of 1.1 billion, about four times as large as it has currently.

In other words, only an astronomical, utterly impractical level of immigration will prevent population aging. Smaller increases have little impact. If immigration were reduced to 200,000 annually – 50,000 less than the current level – 24.8 percent of Canadians would be 65 and older in 2036. Even if immigration intake were boosted to 500,000 – double the current level – the percentage of Canadians 65 and older would still rise substantially, from the current 12 percent to 21.3 percent by 2036. That massive discrepancy in immigration levels – a difference of 300,000 newcomers per year – results in only a small difference in the percentage of Canadians who'll be 65 and older 30-odd years from now.

In either scenario, Canada sees a jump in the percentage of people 65 and older. It is ludicrous to suggest that, given a choice between 17 million immigrants over the next 34 years and 6.8 million, we should opt for 17 million merely to achieve a slightly smaller percentage of people who are 65 and older. Such a step would not make Canada a younger society in any noticeable way. Nor would it improve the economic well-being of Canadians. It would, however, wreak havoc on the cities where immigrants concentrate, cities whose infrastructures are already strained by rapid growth.

Frank Denton, Christine Feaver, and Byron Spencer, the McMaster University scholars who made these projections, concluded that "immigration is clearly not an effective tool for offsetting the process of population aging." Indeed, even the modest population rejuvenation they project is probably exaggerated. The projections assume a constant age distribution of immigrants over the next three decades. That's unlikely to be the case when the rest of the world, including the immigrant-sending countries, is aging too.

The notion of Canada as an aging society has been hugely overstated. From the exaggerated response to the 2001 census data, you'd think people with canes were about to overrun the country. Not so. Canada's older citizens are living longer than ever, but they will not live forever. Even the boomers' reign as the most influential group is coming to an end: by the end of this decade, they and those born before them will be outnumbered by those born since 1966. Like the rest of the world, Canada is getting older because of lower fertility and increased longevity. But older does not mean old; Canada is never going to become a nation of seniors.

THE ECONOMIC MYTH

"Immigrants create jobs," Terence Corcoran writes in the *National Post*. "The only people fuelling the economy are immigrants," Haroon Siddiqui informs us in the *Toronto Star*. Praise for the economic contribution of immigrants is so widespread and effusive, one might almost conclude that Canadian-born people couldn't so much as feed and clothe themselves were it not for the kindness of immigrants in coming over to rescue them.

Contrary to conventional wisdom, Canada does not depend on immigrants for economic growth; it never has. For much of Canada's history, the fastest growth in real per capita incomes occurred at times when net migration (immigration less emigration) was zero or negative. Immigrants create jobs, yes. By their presence, they make the economy larger, increasing the demand for goods and services and for people to make and deliver those goods and services. But they occupy the jobs they create, so the statement "immigrants create jobs" is essentially meaningless. There is no evidence that immigration "creates jobs" in the usual sense of that phrase – that is, reduces unemployment.

Immigration is an emotional subject to which many of us feel a strong personal connection. Perhaps it is because immigration arouses such strong emotions that many people, some journalists included, don't pause to check facts before issuing strong opinions about it. This might explain why commentary in Canadian newspapers on the economic impact of immigration seems to bear no relationship to any of the serious research done on the subject.

It is a mystery why otherwise reliable writers think immigration is an economic boon. No major study, in Canada or elsewhere, has reached that conclusion. If immigration were an economic godsend, it would make everybody richer. It doesn't do that. In 1991, the Economic Council of Canada concluded that immigration had a tiny positive impact on average per capita incomes. A previous Canadian study, for the Macdonald royal commission in 1985, had concluded that immigration actually caused a decline in real per capita incomes and real wages.

In Australia, a three-year study found that the only result of immigration was to make the Australian economy larger; it did nothing for the individuals within that economy. The Australian economists concluded: "There can be little economic justification for moving large numbers of people to Australia from other countries."

Because most studies have found that immigration causes, at most, very small positive or negative impacts on per capita income, economists tend to view the economic impact as neutral. Increasing the population through immigration is like doubling the size of a pie and, at the same time, doubling the number of people who want to eat it.

But there's more to the story than that. To understand the full economic impact of immigration, we must look not just at average incomes but at individual incomes as well. What if one of the original eaters got one and a half pieces after the pie was enlarged, while another received only half a piece? Per capita pie consumption would stay the same, but one eater would be better off at the expense of another.

Thanks to the work of the brilliant American economist George Borjas, we know that redistribution of the pie among members of the host community is precisely what happens because of immigration. Borjas, a professor at Harvard University's Kennedy School of Government, is the leading immigration economist in the United States. As a believer in the benefits of skilled immigration, Borjas has long been a booster of Canada's points system, arguing that, because of it, immigrants to Canada tend to do better on average than their American counterparts.

That's why he was disappointed when I informed him, during a telephone interview, that the skilled portion of Canada's immigration intake was down to 23 percent. "Why did it shrink way down?" he asked from his Harvard office. "Why did the Canadians allow this to occur?"

Because the Canadian program had been taken over by its clientele, I said, who insisted that the family class be expanded (resulting in fewer skilled immigrants). He commiserated. In the United States, all immigration, not just 77 percent of it, is based on family ties. Borjas objects to the family-based system even though, as his critics point out, he himself is a beneficiary of a program that did not require him and his mother to meet a skills test when they arrived in Miami from Cuba in 1962. "I'm not a Cuban when I do economics," he explains.

In his latest book, *Heaven's Door*, Borjas gives us a new way to look at immigration and understand its economic impact. His complex analysis boils down to the old saying "No pain, no gain." Immigration creates additional competition in the labour market, reducing the wages of native workers. The result is a huge transfer of wealth to employers and, to a lesser extent, consumers. The winners win slightly more than the losers lose; so there is an "immigration surplus" that can be seen as a gift from immigrants to the country as a whole. But this gift is very small, which is why many analyses dismiss the economic impact as virtually neutral.

What brings about this "immigration surplus"? Borjas says it's similar to the way a country gains from foreign trade. Suppose the United States imports toys made by low-paid labour overseas. American workers in the toy industry suffer wage cuts and job losses. But the benefits enjoyed by American consumers, in the form of lower toy prices, are somewhat greater than the income lost by American workers.

The same thing happens if, instead of importing toys, the United States imports workers to make the toys there at lower wages than existing workers were earning. "Immigration increases the size of the economic pie available to natives. Immigration also redistributes income – from native workers, who compete with immigrants, to those who hire and use immigrant services. Immigration changes the way the economic pie is split between workers and firms."

Borjas notes the irony that those who stress the benefits of immigration and advocate more open admission policies usually downplay the impact of immigration on native wages. "They are in for a shock," he writes. "There is no immigration surplus if the native wage is not reduced by immigration." Borjas's analysis lets us see the Canadian immigration program for what it is: an income redistribution scheme that benefits the wealthiest members of society. Because the Canadian program is substantial, the resulting income transfer is massive, about $30.7 billion per year.

A continuous influx of new workers enriches employers at the expense of workers already here. This is clearly the most important economic impact of immigration, and yet it's a secret in Canada. Why? The program's supporters on the right never mention it, perhaps because they'd rather it were kept a secret. If it weren't, popular indignation might result in a curtailment of immigration; those on the right – people like Andrew Coyne – want it expanded, presumably to the point where governments would have no choice but to eliminate the minimum wage and disband the welfare state.

Immigration of 850,000 a year, as recommended by Coyne, would represent an influx of new workers so massive as to make minimum wage laws unenforceable. Moreover, it makes no sense to bring in large numbers of workers whose only asset is a willingness to work for low wages while attempting to maintain a minimum wage higher than what employers pay such workers. As for the welfare state, as two other conservative thinkers, Milton Friedman and David Frum, have pointed out, wide-open immigration makes social programs too expensive to maintain.

The political left in Canada – what remains of it – is also silent about the damage our program does to working Canadians. Most immigrants are non-white, so arguing for less immigration smacks of political incorrectness and horrifies many of the New Democratic Party's remaining supporters. The NDP's immigration policy, as a result, is that of the *Wall Street Journal* and other voices of the political right.

The NDP wants higher immigration levels and less selectivity even though that policy, if implemented, would further depress wages, weaken labour unions, and undermine social programs. The policy makes sense for the political right because it boosts corporate profits and makes wealthy people wealthier. But it's a bizarre program to be espoused by a party that deems itself the friend of the working man. The NDP underestimates the intelligence of wage-earning Canadians when it asks them to embrace a policy so blatantly hostile to their own interests.

Unions, which might be expected to defend the interests of working people, are silent on the issue, probably because they, too, are prisoners of political correctness. Professional organizations, such as those representing doctors and engineers, have no such inhibitions about preventing immigrants from competing with their members. Strict certification procedures make it difficult for foreign-trained professionals to practise in Canada.

Borjas has devised a formula to estimate the immigration surplus in any free-market economy. In the United States, he finds that immigration increases the income of the native-born population by $8 billion a year, or $30 per native-born person. In an $8-trillion economy, $8 billion is not much, especially compared with the $152-billion drop in earnings of native-born workers. Gains that wage-earning American consumers receive from immigration are minuscule compared with the money they lose to wage compression.

Applied to Canada, the Borjas formula reveals a loss to native workers of $30.7 billion annually. This is proportionately higher than the lost wages in the United States because Canada has proportionately more immigrants: a foreign-born population of 17 percent, compared with 10 percent south of the border. Users of immigrant services gain approximately $33.8 billion per year because of the presence of immigrants, leaving an immigration surplus of $3.1 billion.

These figures are a rough estimate, but they give a good idea of the scale of immigration's impact on the Canadian economy. It is huge. Enormous sums are transferred from workers to employers because immigration, by increasing the labour force, depresses wages; in return, society as a whole enjoys a modest bonus. Borjas's originality lies in his insight that the benefits of immigration flow from wage losses and his development of a formula for quantifying those losses. His work demonstrates that reducing the price of labour is what immigration, from an economic standpoint, is all about.

That immigration pushes down wages is hardly news. Paul Samuelson, the Nobel Prize–winning economist, had this to say in *Economics*, a textbook familiar to every student who has taken introductory economics: "By keeping labour supply down, a restrictive immigration policy tends to keep wages high."

Alan Greenspan, the powerful chairman of the U.S. Federal Reserve Board, is well aware of immigration's impact on wages. Greenspan's job is to keep the American inflation rate down, and keeping wages down is a good way to do that. Naturally he's a fan of high immigration levels. In a speech in February 2000, he said that unless immigration were "uncapped," worker shortages in the United States would persist and, "short of repeal of the law of supply and demand," wages would rise.

For Greenspan, immigration is good because it limits wage increases, reining in inflation. For the worker whose wages are chopped, it's not good. Immigration is good for some and bad for others. That's why general statements such as the following, from the NDP's platform, are foolish: "Canada has always benefited from the economic boost . . . that immigration brings." In fact, Canada as a whole has not benefited much, though certain interests in Canada have benefited a lot; the biggest winners don't vote for the NDP.

In the same policy paper, the NDP criticizes the Liberals for not raising immigration levels quickly enough. The New Democrats want immigration of 1 percent of the population and they want it now. Did anyone in the NDP study economics? Does this social democratic party actually believe that its platform is good for the Canadian worker it seeks to represent?

Here's what the economists Alan Green and David Green had to say about the Brian Mulroney policy of high immigration: "The winners and losers from the new policy are relatively clear. The biggest loser is labour. Earlier policies that sought to fill occupational gaps tried to ensure that workers did not face direct competition from new immigrants. The current policy brings in workers even if their intended occupation is not in excess demand."

The NDP's response? To urge that levels be made even higher than what the Tories and Liberals already have implemented, thereby increasing the size of the income transfer from workers to employers. This is what happens when policy is based on a false premise – "immigration boosts the economy" – rather than on the more complicated fact: immigration slightly increases the size of the economic pie but the price of that small increase is a big drop in wages.

You needn't be an economist to see signs of the $31-billion immigration income transfer going on around us. Back in the 1970s, as a newspaper reporter in Toronto, I often worked the night shift that the building cleaners worked. I got to know some of them. They were members of the same union that represented the reporters and other newspaper workers. They earned decent salaries, enough to buy houses and raise families. Of how many cleaners today could that be said? Most employers now contract out their cleaning rather than hiring such workers directly. The cleaning firms pay low wages. Many of their employees are new Canadians and members of extended families that live together. They accept very low wages more readily than Canadian-born workers would.

Who wins in this scenario? The customers of the cleaning services, who pay less for those services than they would if Canada did not admit 250,000 mostly unskilled immigrants every year. Who loses? The people who used to clean buildings for a living wage.

In Europe, large underground parking garages in the centres of big cities rarely have human employees. Most have machines that accept money or credit cards and produce a ticket that the driver inserts into another machine at the exit. This kind of technology, common in Europe for the past 15 years, is just beginning to become widespread in Canada. Europe has less immigration – much less available cheap labour – than Canada does. What if Canada had followed the European pattern in this case? New, well-paid jobs for well-trained workers would have been created because people are needed to make, install, and service the parking garage technology. In Canada, however, it's cheaper for garage owners to employ minimum-wage labour than to invest in expensive new machines. The employers win again. The workers – who might have occupied the good jobs that, because of Canada's immigration policy, were not created – are the losers.

Part of immigration mythology is that all job creation is good. In reality, some job creation is good. If a Canadian company needs workers with specialized skills and attracts them from overseas, that is an unmitigated good. The company gets the help it needs; the newcomers exploit their talents because of the opportunity offered in Canada; no one in the pre-existing workforce is harmed because the newcomers' talents were complementary rather than competitive. There are no losers in this scenario, only winners.

But much of the job creation caused by immigration involves unskilled work. Many people who live in Toronto have no skills and cannot speak English. Partly because of this surfeit of unskilled workers, an industry has grown up to deliver advertising flyers door to door. Most householders consider this paper a nuisance, but it's a cost-effective way for supermarkets and other merchants to reach potential customers. Here's the "job creation" lauded by those who advocate large-scale immigration. Were it not for Canada's policy, many flyer delivery jobs would not exist, true enough; but it's hard to see how Canada benefits from the existence of these jobs. In their absence, merchants would find other ways to inform their customers, perhaps by including supplements in daily or weekly papers or by having them delivered by the higher-paid workforce of the post office. The merchants are the winners in this case because they get cheaper advertising. The newspapers, the post office, and their employees are the losers.

The Mulroney-Chrétien policy has two essential characteristics: lots of immigrants and few skilled immigrants. Since it was implemented in the late 1980s, a fast-growing job category in Canada has been that of garment homeworker. Almost all are Asian immigrants. According to the Maquila Solidarity Network, a Canadian organization that promotes improved working conditions for Third World workers, at least 40,000 homeworkers participate in Canada's garment industry. They're part of the underground economy: they do not appear in official statistics; and they have none of the rights and benefits other Canadian workers take for granted, such as statutory holiday pay or unemployment insurance. They work at home or in small, unregulated shops. Most make less than minimum wage, as little as $3 an hour. They are hired and fired as production schedules dictate. Ching, a Toronto homeworker interviewed in a Maquila publication, said, "I know I'm being underpaid, but there is nothing I can do. If I don't do the work, someone else will. The boss knows where to get cheap labour."

In March 2000, the British Columbia Employment Standards Branch launched an investigation into Eminent Knitting Ltd., a Vancouver company that had gone into receivership. Employees alleged that the owner, Eddie Chi Kin Mak, owed them money. The employees, almost all recent immigrants from China, said they had been working 60 to 70 hours a week, sometimes six or seven days a week, for less than minimum wage. Mei Fang, 67, showed the *Vancouver Sun* pay slips that indicated she was paid minimum wage for four hours of work when, in fact, she had worked eight hours or longer. "I would start sometimes at 8.30 a.m.," she said, "and work until 10 at night." Many of the employees were doing piecework, not realizing they were entitled to minimum wage. So they put in the unpaid hours to finish.

Occasionally articles appear in the media deploring sweatshops. Employers should, of course, respect employment laws and the rights of employees. But if the government, by its policy, is going to add thousands of low-skilled workers to the labour market, it's naive to assume that no one is going to find a profitable way to exploit them.

If an economic goal of the Canadian government is to create a world-class sweatshop garment industry to compete with poor countries like Bangladesh, large-scale immigration is ideal. If not, Canada should not import large numbers of people equipped for no other kind of job. First our immigration policy creates the conditions that make the growth of sweatshops inevitable. Then we deplore their existence. It does not make sense, but when politics meets immigration, not much does.

Underpaid home and sweatshop work is just one example of the changes brought about in exchange for the small "immigration surplus" George Borjas identified. It's time to stop arguing over whether immigration makes a country better off, Borjas concludes, because "the net gain seems to be much too small to justify such a grand social experiment. The debate is really over the fact that some people gain substantially, while others lose. In short, the immigration debate is a tug of war between the winners and the losers."

And yet, don't immigrants do the jobs nobody else wants? Those of us in the major cities would be in big trouble if there were no foreign-born Canadians to staff hospitals, drive cabs, and clean houses. Years ago, I put the oft-asked question to Neil Swan, the erudite economist who headed the Economic Council of Canada's landmark study of immigration. He sighed, rolled his eyes, and finally said, "No job ever did not get done if somebody really wanted it done."

Borjas agrees. Immigrants, he says, take jobs that native-born people do not want *at the going wage*. This doesn't mean, however, "that natives would refuse to work in those jobs if the immigrants had never arrived and employers were forced to raise wages to fill the positions."

What would happen if an enlightened government returned to a rational immigration policy – say, 150,000 immigrants per year – and the supply of cleaning ladies were reduced? Some might raise their price from, say, $80 to $120 a day. That would encourage others, including Canadian-born ones, to enter the market, perhaps pushing the rate back down to $100. The lawyer who employs a cleaner would have to shell out more. The income gap between lawyer and cleaner would narrow slightly. Similarly, there would be greater equality of income between people who take taxis and those who drive them.

It's clear why proponents of the right, who think wage inflation is worse than income inequality, don't want to see cleaning ladies and cab drivers earn more. But it's weird that so many Canadians, who pride themselves on their social consciences and progressive politics, hurl nasty names at those who call for a more limited immigration program. The left, in its innocence, seems to think it's an anomaly that the Mulroney government opened the gates to massive immigration and that this policy is supported by prominent conservatives. It's no anomaly. The right knows exactly what it's doing when it lines up behind Canada's program and lobbies for even higher levels of immigration. It's the left that hasn't a clue.

CHAPTER SIX

THE ILLUSION OF MULTICULTURALISM

GABRIEL YIU, A VANCOUVER FLOWER MERCHANT AND A former columnist for *Ming Pao*, a daily newspaper, was speaking not long ago with a visiting Chinese scholar. "Why," the scholar wanted to know, "is there no dog on the menu in any of the Chinese restaurants in Vancouver? I thought Canada was a multicultural country."

Yiu couldn't come up with a good answer. Like most Canadians, he'd been taught to think of Canada as a multicultural country. The reality, and the answer to the visitor's question, is that while Canada has a diverse urban population, it is not multicultural. The absence of dog from the menus of Chinese restaurants is only one example – perhaps too graphic an example for some – of how this is so.

We learn in school that Canada is a mosaic, not an American-style melting pot. A mosaic consists of tiles, each one separate, that together form a pattern. If each of Canada's multiple ethnic groups is a part of a mosaic, what happens within that part should not be any business of someone who lives in one of the other parts. The visiting scholar had a point.

Many Chinese from mainland China (though not those from Hong Kong) are dog eaters. So are Koreans who, in Korea, frequent specialty dog restaurants that offer such delicacies as "tonic soup." Korean men believe dog meat enhances sexual prowess and have been eating it for centuries. Here dogs are doted upon as part of the family. It's deeply offensive (as well as illegal) in Western countries to sell dog meat. But from the Chinese or Korean viewpoint, there seems no logical reason why it would be acceptable to eat cow, pig, chicken, and lamb but not dog.

Canadian dog lovers, if they really believed in multiculturalism, would respect the right of other cultures to be different. They could be faithful to their own culture by steering clear of restaurants with poodles on the menu. So why can't the Chinese and Korean parts of the Canadian mosaic fully express their culinary cultures? Because all hell would break loose. Dog lovers are passionate and uncompromising. Politicians can yak all they want about multiculturalism, they would say, but this is Canada and nobody had better eat any dogs. Korean-style dog restaurants would need armed guards.

Canadian leaders, from Governor General Adrienne Clarkson on down, use the words "diversity" and "multiculturalism" as if they were synonymous. They're not, and this linguistic misuse is responsible for much of the confusion over cultural differences among Canadians. Diversity encompasses a broad range of characteristics that differentiate people: religion, language, dress, leisure pursuits, and so forth. Diversity is not divisive in a secular Western democracy that upholds the freedom of the individual. But because there are irreconcilable differences between cultures, multiculturalism is divisive. That's why Canadians don't care what people eat – until someone decides to barbecue man's best friend. It's why Canadians don't care what people wear – until an RCMP member demands the right to wear a turban, changing a uniform that's a national symbol.

Some immigrants bring attitudes that are unacceptable to the majority of Canadians and, in some cases, illegal. Just as Canadian Muslims have no right to kill Salman Rushdie, Muslims who emigrate from Africa lose the right to have their daughters circumcised. Men in Canada do not have the right to have more than one wife at a time, even if the culture they brought with them says they do. And they have no right to beat their wives and children or to force a daughter to marry someone she does not want to. Filipino immigrants have no right to stage the cockfights that entertained them at home.

Newcomers might be excused for wondering why they don't have these rights. Why, they might ask, do Canada's leaders boast about its multiculturalism if they do not want the country actually to be multicultural? The answer is that Canada's leaders are hypocrites. As with every aspect of the immigration program, there is the official version and the real version. In the official version, Canada is unlike other countries, such as Britain and France, that also have diverse populations but do not have official multiculturalism. Canada, so the story goes, has found a new model for social harmony by encouraging immigrants to maintain their own cultures rather than expecting them to assimilate into ours.

The reality is quite different. Perhaps that's why two of the most insightful books on the subject of Canadian multiculturalism both have the word "illusion" in their titles. Neil Bissoondath, a novelist of Indian background who was born in Trinidad and now lives in Quebec, thought he was going to become a Canadian when he moved to Canada. He had no intention of becoming an Indo-Trinidadian-Canadian and he wrote a book, *Selling Illusions: The Cult of Multiculturalism in Canada*, explaining why.

In *The Illusion of Difference*, the University of Toronto sociologists Raymond Breton and Jeffrey Reitz examined the widely held belief that Canada is a mosaic in which immigrants retain their identities – unlike the United States, a melting pot in which immigrants swiftly become unhyphenated Americans. They found that, in fact, immigrants to Canada assimilate as quickly as do immigrants to the United States and, indeed, that Canadians are even less inclined than Americans to favour retention of ethnic cultural differences.

Canada's immigration program is based, as we've seen, on demonstrably false claims of economic and demographic necessity. Multiculturalism, an offshoot of our immigration program, consists of rhetoric similarly disconnected from the real world. Hypocrisy is a poor foundation for public policy because it can't help but sow confusion and cynicism.

Khat provides a classic example. I first heard about khat (pronounced "cot") while researching a magazine article about Somali refugee claimants who had settled in Toronto. It was obvious that drug dealing was going on around some suburban apartment buildings favoured by Somalis. It wasn't the usual drugs that were being sold but a leaf known as khat, from a shrub that grows in East Africa and on the Arabian peninsula. The leaf, which resembles rhubarb, is chewed for its euphoric effects, similar to those provided by amphetamines. Khat is used by Somalis as a social lubricant, the way Western people use wine or beer. It's also an important part of weddings and other festive gatherings.

At the time, it was illegal to import khat but legal to possess it. Health Canada has since banned it altogether. (Khat is also illegal in the United States and most European countries, but not Britain.) The active ingredients are prohibited under the Canada Health and Safety Act, following a recommendation of the World Health Organization. In the United States, cathinone, one of the plant's components, is classified as a schedule I controlled substance, a category that includes LSD, heroin, and ecstasy. Health Canada says khat can cause high blood pressure, cardiac problems, hallucination, and insanity. The Somalis I've talked to say it makes people happy and helps conversation to flow. Some Somalis think the prohibition is simply an excuse for the police to harass them.

What to do about khat? The answer depends on one's view of drugs, and of multiculturalism. Many recreational drugs are illegal in Canada. If you think we should lighten up about drugs, you probably favour lifting the ban on khat. If you think not, you would probably leave it, along with LSD and ecstasy, as a banned substance.

From the perspective of multiculturalism, it's a more interesting issue. My own view is that Canada isn't a multicultural country and that real attempts to make it one would cause severe social discord. As for the Somalis, nobody forced them to come here. They came as refugee claimants even though most had already obtained safety elsewhere. For that reason, Canada was under no moral or legal obligation to admit them. Why did they come? Many came because Canada is the easiest place to get welfare, a fact known even in remote parts of Africa and Asia. Easy welfare is part of the "pull factor" that draws refugee claimants to Canada.

By admitting the Somalis and supporting them financially, Canada has bestowed huge favours on them. Now they think Canada's drug laws should be adapted to their social customs? I don't see why, but then I'm not a multiculturalist. If multiculturalism were more than an empty word, its adherents would surely support the Somalis' right to use khat. The dominant culture in Canada makes extensive use of alcohol, but practising Muslims, as many Somalis are, may not use alcohol. If Canada were truly a mosaic, the Somalis would be able to use their intoxicant of choice. But it's not a true mosaic, and the majority culture's emphasis on health and safety supersedes the culture of a minority group.

Canada is officially multicultural; France is officially unicultural. Both countries have banned khat. The French give the Somalis a clear message: "You're in France, so you have to do things our way. If you want to chew khat, you must leave. We don't allow that here." The Canadians' message is mixed and mystifying: "We are officially multicultural and proud of it. We wouldn't dream of asking you to abandon your Somali culture, which makes up a valuable part of our mosaic. Oh, and by the way, if you chew khat, we'll put you in jail." To the Somalis, the difference between the French and the Canadians is simply that the French are honest about where they stand while the Canadians aren't. Meanwhile, in non-multicultural Britain, you can buy khat in grocery stores.

In another safety-versus-culture case, a Sikh went to the British Columbia Human Rights Commission to argue that he should be exempt from the law requiring motorcyclists to wear helmets because his religion required him to wear a turban instead. And there have been other cases of the Sikh dress code clashing with Canadian norms. The most famous happened when a controversy erupted after the Royal Canadian Mounted Police granted a Sikh officer's request that he be allowed to wear his turban on duty.

This episode was seen as a victory for multiculturalism; in retrospect, it looks more like a defeat. It showed that the official line about Canada being a multicultural paradise was a lie. The case was a reality check for the ideologues of multiculturalism, who had convinced themselves there was no such thing as a Canadian culture (a Liberal multiculturalism minister, Sheila Finestone, actually said this) or national symbols that Canadians cared about.

In Canada, dress is a matter of individual choice, in contrast to theocratic Muslim countries in which dress codes are forced on the population. Few Canadians would suggest that an orthodox Sikh doctor, bus driver, or store clerk should be denied the right to wear a turban. The RCMP case became a cultural issue, and therefore divisive, because the RCMP, especially in western Canada, is a cherished institution. Moreover, it is a quasi-military organization, and military organizations everywhere require their members to wear identical uniforms. The commissioner of the RCMP sided with the Sikh.

The Sikh Mountie was not merely practising diversity but was challenging deeply felt beliefs of a large segment of the majority culture. A group of retired officers took up the challenge. In federal court they argued that the turban infringed their constitutional right to a secular state free of religious symbols. A petition with an impressive total of 210,000 names backed them up. The court, in ruling in favour of the RCMP, rejected the claim of Sikh organizations that not allowing the turban would amount to religious discrimination. Instead, it upheld the right of the RCMP to change its uniform code.

The Sikhs won but they paid a price – one that most minority groups would prefer to avoid. Many Canadians were embittered by the turban episode and still are. Their message to the ethnic communities was clear: there are limits to how much multiculturalism Canadians will swallow, and if you push those limits, there will be trouble. As it turned out, the RCMP case settled nothing. In March 2002, a Montreal school board ruled that a 12-year-old boy could not wear his religious dagger, or kirpan, because it violated the rule against dangerous objects.

Turbans on Mounties, a leaf chewed by Somalis, the dietary habits of Chinese and Koreans – aren't these rather trivial matters? Perhaps they are, but multiculturalism itself isn't trivial. It touches on such fundamental concepts as separation of church and state, equality of women, and the rights of children. To many immigrants, these are radical, alien concepts, difficult to accept. If Canada is multicultural, some of them believe, maybe they shouldn't have to accept them.

A judge once told me that men who appeared before her charged with assaulting their wives or girlfriends had argued that their culture gave them licence to do so. She did not accept the arguments, but other judges have accepted similar defences. In 1994, a Quebec judge gave a man 23 months in jail, instead of the four years the prosecution requested, for repeatedly sodomizing his 11-year-old stepdaughter. She justified the light sentence on the grounds that, given the man's Islamic faith, he should be given some credit for preserving the girl's virginity. Muslims were as outraged as other Canadians by the judge's suggestion that the man's religion in some way mitigated his actions.

In February 2002, an Ontario couple were arrested for having their 11-year-old daughter circumcised. This practice, involving removal of the clitoris, is widespread in Africa and parts of Asia but illegal in the West. With its official multiculturalism, Canada confuses people who come here, who are urged to retain their cultures and then jailed for doing so. Female circumcision is an important part of the culture of many countries; the United Nations estimates 2 million such procedures are performed annually. "Culturally, fathers and mothers think it's a good thing for their girls," Nadia Badr of the Sudanese Women Association of Niagara told the *National Post*. "They have no idea it's wrong."

At about the same time, a murder trial involving a horrific case of child abuse was unfolding in Toronto. The father of the brutalized little boy said that, in Jamaica, parents have the right to "whip" their children – the multiculturalism defence. How many girls have suffered genital mutilation in Canada, losing a lifetime of sexual pleasure, because immigrants believed Canada's official policy gave them the right to practise their culture? How many children have been beaten under the imprimatur of multiculturalism?

Because of multiculturalism, there is more overt hostility in Canada to those of European ancestry (who made up 87 percent of the population, as of the 1996 census) than to the non-white minority. In the name of multiculturalism, the achievements of Canada's founders have been all but eradicated from school books. Multiculturalists believe English-Canadian schoolchildren should not be allowed to have English historical heroes. Yet, as Richard Gwyn, writing of the demise of English-Canadian nationalism, says, "It was English-Canadians who explored the greater part of the country, cleared it, and settled it. It was they who contributed the overwhelming majority of men who died fighting in wars for democracy and freedom. It was they who created almost all of the country's political and legal infrastructure."

They also opened Canada up to immigrants from all over the world and passed laws outlawing racism and discrimination. And what do they get in return? From Jean Chrétien they get multiculturalism ministers who belittle the English-Canadian culture and vilify them as cross-burning racists.

It's doubtful that Pierre Trudeau intended multiculturalism to become such a nasty business when he enshrined the policy in law in 1971 – although, as Neil Bissoondath pointed out, the Act for the Preservation and Enhancement of Multiculturalism in Canada was notable for its "lack of any mention of unity." Instead, it aimed at "ensuring that the various ethnic groups whose interests it espouses discover no compelling reason to blur the distinctions among them."

Trudeau's multiculturalism act marked the first time in history that a country had deliberately set out to heighten, intensify, and make permanent the ethnic differences among its people. Why would Canada do this to itself? In part, the policy was a response to the Royal Commission on Bilingualism and Biculturalism, which had recommended a two-nations policy – one French, one English – for Canada. At the time, this was also the policy of the Progressive Conservatives under Robert Stanfield.

Trudeau hated the two-nations idea. He envisioned a bilingual Canada with no special status for Quebec. Multiculturalism, as Gwyn points out in *The Northern Magus*, his biography of Trudeau, was a way of forestalling biculturalism. Trudeau seemed to think that French-Canadians would become just another hyphenated group among dozens of others. It didn't work as planned, Gwyn writes, because "French-Canadians escaped easily from the thicket of hyphens Trudeau was trying to plant amongst them by renaming themselves Québécois."

If anything, the Québécois were strengthened by multiculturalism, if only because English Canada was weakened by it. By dividing Canadians outside Quebec into dozens of hyphenated groups, multiculturalism amounted to a systematic attempt to eliminate the national identity of English-speaking Canada. In contrast, Quebec's national identity has been reinforced, in part through changes to the immigration program that gave it the right to enhance its francophone character by recruiting francophone immigrants. English Canada has no right to use immigration to enhance its character.

In the 1972 election, Trudeau squeaked back into power with only a two-seat advantage over the Conservatives. Demoted to minority status in Parliament, Trudeau decided to switch his approach from doing what was right to doing what worked. He had to be prepared, Gwyn writes, "to use every tool and all the money in the public purse to win re-election." Trudeau had been accused of neglecting the ethnic vote. That wouldn't do. And so, recounts Gwyn, "up sprang a trebled multiculturalism program that functioned as a slush fund to buy votes."

As an answer to Quebec nationalism, multiculturalism was a flop. Its real value, the Liberals saw, was as part of their electoral machinery. In 2002, with the federal opposition in such disarray that Canada is effectively a one-party state, it's easy to forget that the Liberals' hold on power has, more often than not, been tenuous. The Liberals know the time will come when that hold becomes tenuous again. Immigration and multiculturalism are life rafts on the Liberal ship. They exist to carry a core group of ethnic constituencies that are supposed to prevent the party from sinking whenever it finds itself in rough waters.

After the near defeat of 1972, Trudeau's government began funding dozens of organizations that claimed to represent ethnic Canadians. Some were created for the sole purpose of obtaining these grants. Many were unknown to the people they claimed to represent. A 1976 evaluation of ethnic organizations getting government money found the typical one had only 20 to 85 members.

An umbrella group, the Canadian Ethnocultural Council, claimed to speak for millions of Canadians yet was almost entirely dependent on the government for support. So were the groups within it. In a 1994 study, John Bryden, a dissident Liberal MP, found that the National Association of Canadians of Origins in India, which claimed to speak for 750,000 Canadians, had raised only $4,900 through memberships and donations, relying on the government for the $68,000 it needed to exist. The Liberals were using public money to create a caste of professional multiculturalists dependent on the government for their jobs. In return for their wages, these people were expected to help swing their communities behind the Liberals.

How to sell this crude vote-buying program to the public? Trudeau, with characteristic audacity, argued that multiculturalism would enhance national unity. How so? National unity "must be founded on confidence in one's own individual identity; out of this can grow respect for others and a willingness to share ideas, attitudes, and assumptions."

Like many of Trudeau's statements, this sounded reasonable until you thought about it carefully. Of course people should have confidence in their own identity and respect for others. But where was the evidence that they needed help from Ottawa to build that confidence? And by what bizarre logic could organizations created at taxpayers' expense to reinforce ethnic divisions be seen as contributing to national unity?

Laura Sabia, a prominent feminist and author, was not fooled. In a 1978 speech she attacked politicians "whose motto is 'divide and rule.' I, for one, refuse to be hyphenated. I am a Canadian, first and foremost." Judging from opinion polls, Sabia, like Bissoondath, spoke for the majority. Canadians wanted to be Canadians, not Italian-Canadians or Indo-Canadians. But the newly empowered multiculturalists were determined to give them hyphens whether they wanted hyphens or not. In multicultural Canada, you can be British-Canadian or Sikh-Canadian or Finnish-Canadian, but you can't be Canadian. Your ethnicity resides in the word before the hyphen; the "Canadian" signifies only citizenship, not ethnicity.

From an anthropological view, these distinctions make no sense. And a growing number of Canadians don't agree with them. In a 1991 Angus Reid survey, 63 percent of respondents, told they could choose only one answer for their identity, chose Canadian. Only 13 percent of those born in Canada identified themselves by some other ethnic origin, and only 33 percent born elsewhere chose an ethnic identity other than Canadian.

In 1996, for the first time, Statistics Canada included "Canadian" as an ethnicity option on the census form. A total of 30.9 percent indicated Canadian as their sole or partial ethnic origin. As the idea of Canadian ethnicity gains acceptance, that percentage can be expected to grow. This is a triumph of common sense over official policy.

Ideas about race and ethnicity have evolved in recent decades. Only 60 years ago, Hitler unleashed a world war motivated in part by theories of race that seem insane today but were widely accepted then. Hitler thought the "Aryan race" was superior to others. There is no such thing as an Aryan "race." Nor is there an English or a French "race." Even the standard division of mankind into Asian, black, and Caucasian "races" is under scientific challenge because the genetic differences among these groups are so small.

If ethnicity is not biological – and science tells us it is not – then it can only be linguistic, geographical, and cultural. Anyone who was born in English-speaking Canada or has lived in it for a long time, speaks English fluently, and accepts Canadian values has every reason to identify herself or himself as an ethnic Canadian. And the rapid growth in the number of

Canadians with mixed ancestries – 36 percent of the population as of 1996 – can only accelerate this trend. If your grandparents were Italian, Swedish, American, and Japanese, you might as well call yourself Canadian. And since diversity is one of Canada's cultural characteristics, there's no reason why an ethnic Canadian would not have Asian features or black skin or wear a hijab.

Not far from my home in central Toronto is a cluster of Korean restaurants, nightclubs, and shops. It attracts young people who travel in groups and speak Korean among themselves. This is normal because most of them came to Canada relatively recently, and Korean is their first language. But occasionally I encounter young second-generation Koreans in shops or restaurants. Their English, in both accent and vocabulary, is indistinguishable from that of other Canadians. If they grew up in Korean-speaking homes, they probably speak some Korean as well. The chances that *their* children will speak Korean, however, are slim.

Language is much more than a way of communicating; it is a way of thinking, of organizing perception, of looking at the world. It's the basis of cultural identity. If you don't have Korean language, you don't have much Korean culture. Canada's multi-culturalists know this, which is why language is their preoccu-pation. Millions of dollars are spent on heritage language programs aimed at teaching ancestral languages to the descen-dants of immigrants. Extreme multiculturalists would go further. A professor at York University, Evelyn Kallen, once proposed that Canada should become a truly multilingual society and that, to accomplish this, all children should be edu-cated in their ancestral languages. In her version of Canada, English and French would have no special status.

Of course, the chances of anything like this happening are zero. Even if a government were crazy enough to try to imple-ment such a policy, few immigrants would want anything to do with it. But this professor's proposal goes to the heart of what multiculturalism is all about.

Canada's diversity is nothing new; the country has accepted immigrants for much of its history. The linguistic history of past immigrant families is identical to what is happening to the Koreans in my neighbourhood. A first-generation immigrant speaks whatever language he brought to Canada. His children – second-generation Canadians – may speak some of that language, but not as well as their native tongue, English. The third generation – the grandchildren of the original immigrant – are almost always unilingual English-speakers. They may have a smattering of old-country words to make Grandpa chuckle, but not enough to carry on a conversation.

With its heritage language programs and its lofty rhetoric about cultural preservation, official multiculturalism attempts to modify this process. The descendants of immigrants are urged to speak their ancestral languages as well as English. This is a worthy goal; in an ideal world, everyone would be multilingual. Not only does learning other languages make one more educated and tolerant and more receptive to the world, there is some evidence it may even make one's brain work better.

The problem is that kids will learn a language only if they see a need for it. Without that need, they won't expend the effort. The issue then becomes whether public funds should be spent on a project doomed to failure. The sociologists Reitz and Breton merely confirm the obvious: fewer than 1 percent of third-generation Canadians speak an ancestral language other than English or French. Which shows that, despite official multiculturalism, assimilation is happening as rapidly as ever.

To most Canadians, including most foreign-born Canadians, this assimilation is a good thing; to multiculturalists it is appalling. I once heard a prominent ethnic bureaucrat describe an immigrant who opposed multiculturalism as an "assimilationist." The venom with which he spat out the word was striking, as if an assimilationist belonged to the same category of repulsive humankind as, say, a pedophile.

If Canada's professional multiculturalists had their way, Germany's immigration system would be replicated here. German society has been unwilling to accept people of other nationalities as Germans. Three million Turkish guest workers have remained Turks rather than become Germans. Sadly, the situation is getting worse instead of better. The German-language skills of German-born children of Turkish parents have been declining in recent years; these children enter school not knowing any German. That's what happens when assimilation is a dirty word.

Ronald Leung once invited his radio listeners to voice their opinions on multiculturalism. Once was enough. Leung did not get to be the most popular talk-show host among people in the Vancouver area who listen to Chinese-language radio by choosing topics nobody wants to talk about. "No one who calls my program has any interest in multiculturalism, except those in the business of multiculturalism," he told me. "I opened the line and nobody called in except the usual people." Leung's Cantonese-speaking listeners don't want to talk about multiculturalism because they are not interested in a government program, created for partisan purposes, that has little to do with anything that matters in their lives.

As of 2002, there are about 400,000 ethnic Chinese in British Columbia, out of a total population of 3.9 million. Of those, 260,000 speak a Chinese language as their mother tongue. Some 90 percent of them live in Greater Vancouver, where a quarter of the population lists Chinese as its mother tongue, a figure that does not include many non-Chinese-speaking people of Chinese ancestry whose families have been in B.C. for generations.

Canada's vaunted diversity is hardly unique. Visitors to major cities in the United States, France, Britain, and many other Western countries will hear many languages in the streets, encounter people in non-Western dress, observe places of worship of different faiths, and see exotic foods in grocery stores. But just as Canada makes a fuss about slower population growth, which the rest of the world sees as normal and manageable, so too does it get unduly excited about diversity.

We call it multiculturalism and claim it makes us different from all other countries. But the truth is that we're not different. As we have seen, if a practice of the minority culture clashes with an important value of the majority culture, we usually don't allow it, just as the Americans or the French wouldn't allow it.

Take the issue of trees, about which people on the West Coast have especially strong feelings. Vancouverites love their stately cedars, some of which soar 200 feet. When large numbers of wealthy Hong Kong Chinese settled on the west side of Vancouver in the 1980s and 1990s, a fight erupted over trees and houses. Immigrants knocked down the old houses and put up huge new ones, "monster houses" to the locals, often made of brick. That was bad enough, but knocking down ancient trees was worse. For many people, these trees had an almost spiritual significance and nobody had a right to knock them down. It wasn't that the Hong Kong people disliked trees; they simply had their own culture with its own belief system. One such belief is that having a tree in front of your house is bad luck; it could make you poor. An immigrant-versus-native battle ensued, and a new bylaw was passed restricting the rights of homeowners to cut down trees.

Multiculturalism policy will never make Canada truly multicultural. Only immigration policy could achieve that. If an "ethnic" community becomes larger than the European-descended community, it will grow more assertive. It will see no reason to defer to a culture that has fewer adherents than its own. It might change the local bylaw so that it can cut down as many trees as it wants. It might want offices and schools to close on its holidays and to remain open on holidays it doesn't celebrate. It might decide to make its language official and have it spoken in the legislature, placed on all public signs, and compulsory in schools.

If that happened, Canada would finally have what it claims to want: true multiculturalism. If it happens anywhere in Canada, it will be in B.C., and it will be the Chinese community that makes it happen, not because its members are power-hungry but because Ottawa's immigration policy will have made them the dominant group, and it is in the nature of dominant groups to exert dominance.

In the late 1980s, the government of Brian Mulroney began a social experiment on a grand scale by dumping the immigration policy that had evolved in Canada since World War II. The jettisoned policy had worked rather well. Its high degree of public acceptance was signalled by the fact that immigration was rarely discussed in Parliament or the media. It was one of those boring government functions – like the management of lighthouses or the mint – that people assumed were in good hands. Annual changes in immigration levels were of no more interest than annual changes in the production of $5 bills. The government could be counted on to provide what was needed.

When Mulroney's government replaced the old policy with a new one, unique in the world, it transformed urban Canada. It did so without ever announcing it was doing it, without explaining why it was doing it, and without asking the Canadian people whether they wanted it done. Chrétien continues Mulroney's grand social experiment. Nobody in government, the universities, or anywhere else knows what its ultimate impact on Canada will be. With immigration, we're in uncharted waters.

Historically, immigrants have come in waves. A wave would start gradually, pick up force until it crashed on the shore, then recede. In the past, Canada welcomed waves of Ukrainians, Italians, Hungarians, and many others. Often they came over a relatively short period. The Ukrainians who came during the second decade of the 20th century were quickly cut off from their homeland. Communications were poor, travel was slow, and few could have afforded to go back even had they wanted to. When that wave of immigration stopped, and no new Ukrainians came, they were even more cut off. Canada was now their world.

Thanks to Mulroney, immigrants no longer come in waves from a wide variety of places. Most come in a continuous, relentless flow from relatively few countries. The Liberals set the stage for this in 1978 when they allowed immigrants to sponsor working-age parents, thereby facilitating chain immigration, as described in chapter 4.

This had little immediate impact because, under Trudeau, the annual intake of immigrants remained moderate. Then Mulroney increased immigration to 250,000 a year and made this world-beating level permanent, so that there could be no respite ever, even during a recession. Permanent high levels gave momentum to unskilled, family-class immigration, so that one relative could sponsor another, who could sponsor another, who could sponsor another, in an ever-lengthening chain. That's why Vancouver and Toronto have shopping malls and high schools where Chinese is the first language and English is rarely heard.

Canada's intake is not nearly as diverse as is often claimed. There are 192 countries in the world but, in 1999, 55 percent of new immigrants came from only 10 of those countries. Some countries with huge populations, such as Indonesia, Nigeria, and Brazil, send almost no immigrants to Canada. Why? Because it is difficult to get into Canada as an independent immigrant. It is easy to get in if you're sponsored, but few Indonesians or Nigerians have anyone in Canada to sponsor them.

By contrast, huge numbers of potential sponsors from China, India, and Pakistan are already in Canada. As a result, people from these countries (and a few others) have effectively appropriated Canada's immigration program. Barring the advent of a government with the courage to reclaim immigration from the stakeholders, this situation will be permanent, for the ranks of these émigré communities are swelled daily by new arrivals.

Because of modern travel and communications, new arrivals are no longer cut off from their homelands. It is now possible for a recent immigrant from Hong Kong to live in Richmond, a suburb south of Vancouver, almost as if she had never left home. Perhaps she watches the latest Chinese video release while chatting on her cellphone with her husband, who's back in Hong Kong, where he spends most of his time although he is a Canadian citizen. She's also in phone and e-mail contact with friends back home.

Her neighbours speak Cantonese. At the local shopping mall, she buys the same products she bought in Hong Kong. Her lack of English is not a problem. She may never learn much English, but first-generation immigrants, especially homemakers and older people, often don't. That's normal. Her Canadian-born children may not be learning English either, and that's not normal.

New immigrants of the same language group have always tended to gather in neighbourhoods. What's novel is the scale of these immigrant communities – Richmond is 40 percent Chinese – and the fact that the wave of immigrants never recedes. If the flow of immigrants from China never ends (and with 20,000 new arrivals every year in Vancouver, it shows no sign of ending), how big will the new Chinese-speaking communities grow? Will the Canadian-born children in these communities consider themselves Canadians or Chinese people living in Canada? Will these children learn English? Nobody knows the answers, least of all the politicians, long since booted out of office, who began this social experiment.

If anyone can answer the linguistic questions, it would be Lee Gunderson, head of the Department of Language and Literacy Education at University of British Columbia's Faculty of Education. An expert on language acquisition by immigrants, he recently completed a book, *The Achievement of Immigrant Students in English-Only Schools*, based on 12 years of research and interviews with 417 students in Vancouver schools. (The book is due to be published in late 2002.) Gunderson's findings make clear that the Mulroney-Chrétien immigration program – a relentless influx of large numbers of immigrants coming from the same places and going to the same places – has serious implications for language acquisition.

When my own daughter was seven, our family spent a year in the south of France. She did not speak a word of French and was plunked into the equivalent of grade 2 in a local primary school where nobody spoke English. She was desperate to communicate, and within weeks she was doing so. In a few months she was speaking French fluently, and she still speaks it well more than 20 years later. Gunderson agrees with me that, had she attended an English school during that year in France, she probably would not have learned French. Kids learn a new language because they need to, not because some adult says it's good for them.

Many of the ethnic Chinese and East Indian kids in Vancouver, including ones born in Canada, are not as fortunate as my daughter was. Though they live in an English-speaking country and attend English-language schools, they don't need to learn a new language to communicate with the other kids. In one Lower Mainland school, 99 percent of the students are Punjabi. Why would they bother trying to speak English to one another? Even if they did, what sort of English would they learn?

In other Richmond schools, large groups of both Cantonese- and Mandarin-speakers speak those languages among themselves. If a Mandarin-speaker were to speak with a Cantonese-speaker, it would have to be in English, Gunderson says. But students from different language groups rarely interact. "For language acquisition, it's very serious," Gunderson points out.

"I know kindergartens in Vancouver and Richmond where there may be one native English-speaker. The rest are Cantonese-speakers or Mandarin-speakers."

If the English-speaking toddler is outgoing, maybe she'll learn some Cantonese. Otherwise, she'll be isolated. And the only English the Cantonese-speaking kids will hear is from the teacher. That's not nearly as effective as learning English from native English-speaking children. This linguistic mess, created by reckless mismanagement of the immigration program, turns immigrant language acquisition upside down.

"The whole field of English as a second language [ESL] instruction is based on the notion that the language of the community is the target language," Gunderson explains. "It doesn't work any more in many school situations, because the language of the community is not English. We're now in a situation of teaching English as a foreign language rather than English as a second language. That's the way you learn English in China, where the surrounding language is not English."

In interviews with ESL students, Gunderson found they were distressed about not being immersed in English. "The irony," he says, "is that students in an English-only school system found it impossible for various reasons to interact with English-speakers. A majority reported that it was impossible to talk to English-speakers or to hear English spoken." One ESL student told Gunderson, "There are too many Chinese." Nobody could call him racist, since he's a Cantonese-speaking immigrant himself. This boy was worried that he would never learn "proper English" because he never heard it; all he heard in the halls and in the schoolyard was Cantonese. Other immigrants are also affected. A 14-year-old Spanish-speaking boy told Gunderson: "Too much Chinese. ESL classes are fill with Chinese. Teachers no good, not stop Chinese talk."

In Vancouver, some ESL students were born in Canada. This is of increasing concern to teachers, Gunderson says. "Teachers are beginning to say, 'My God, this child was born in Canada and can't speak a word of English. What's going on here?'"

If a German-born child enters school in Germany not speaking German, many Germans view the matter with concern. When Canadian-born children enter school not speaking English, nobody, other than teachers in the privacy of their staff rooms, says anything. Again, it's because the official orthodoxy is that immigration brings only benefits. To point out obvious problems or shortcomings in a ruined immigration program is in bad taste. Those who question the orthodoxy risk being called nasty names by the stakeholders.

What is not said, but should be, is that in parts of Canada we're seeing the introduction of a German-style immigration system: isolation rather than integration. Once again, this creates winners and losers. The winners are British Columbia real estate developers who make fortunes building houses for the new arrivals. The losers are the students, native English-speakers as well as foreign-language-speakers, whose school experience is diminished as a result of the government's social experiment.

The advent of German-style segregation is not happening because the host community does not wish to accept the new-comers; nor is it the result of standoffishness on the part of the immigrants themselves. Rather, it's happening because the volume and concentration of immigration is so great that integration is impeded. If the flow of new immigrants were more limited and diverse, the problem would disappear.

What will happen to a Canadian-born child who grows up in a Chinese-speaking enclave and enters school as an ESL student not speaking English? Because he's immersed in Cantonese or Mandarin rather than English, his progress in what should be his native language is bound to be slow. At the end of 12 years in the school system, will he speak English like the native Canadian he is, with the same command as other Canadian-born people? If not, once he emerges onto the job market, he'll find that poor communications skills are a crippling handicap. "It's a question we can't yet answer," says Gunderson. "We don't know."

So we find ourselves in uncharted waters. The immigration system is so badly broken that it may no longer be capable of integrating newcomers. Multiculturalists in Vancouver may be getting what they want, though not, ironically, because of our policy of multiculturalism. It's our ill-managed immigration program that's causing some Canadian-born people to retain their ancestral language and speak it better than they speak what should be their native language, English. Previously, this has happened only with small religious groups, such as the Yiddish-speaking ultra-Orthodox Jews in Montreal's Outremont area, who deliberately isolate themselves from the surrounding community.

There's only one way deficient English in a second-generation Canadian would not be a handicap. If Vancouver ever got genuine multiculturalism, Chinese would be as common as English in the life of the city. If that happened, a native-born Vancouverite who spoke minimal English with a strong Chinese accent would feel no more out of place than an anglophone in Montreal who speaks poor French.

This may be the eventual outcome of the social experiment Canada has embarked on, but there's a way to go yet. More than half the immigrants to Greater Vancouver speak Cantonese, Mandarin, or Punjabi, but others come from a variety of places. There are still places where immigration works the way it should. At Vancouver's Brock Elementary School, for example, there are 49 first languages among the pupils. Since none is dominant, the language in the halls and on the playground is English. All the kids learn English quickly and pick up some useful multilingual skills as well. "The first thing they learn," chuckles Gunderson, "is how to swear in lots of different languages."

While many schoolchildren are losers in the current program, Vancouver's Chinese community looks like a winner.

Chinese people tell me that they once felt they were just another minority group, and now they feel like "part of the mainstream." That's what constituting almost half the population in a large city will do for you.

Forty years ago, most ethnic Chinese ran restaurants, grocery stores, or laundries. Most lived in the old Chinatown, centred on Pender Street, where everyone, Chinese or not, went for Chinese food. Today Chinese people are more likely to be in business or the professions. They live all over the city and Chinese restaurants are all over the city. That's what people mean when they say they are part of the mainstream, and the change has happened in a generally harmonious fashion. Immigration changes Canada, but Canada changes immigrants, too. After a few years here, a Chinese immigrant is less likely to want to knock down a tree. He may have learned to appreciate its beauty, and he may have learned that it enhances the value of his property.

To the chagrin of politicians who think immigrants should vote for the party that let them in, Vancouver's Chinese community is getting too big and diverse to be manipulated by any political party. At one time you could win a heavily Chinese riding by fielding a Chinese candidate. That's no longer the case. Gabriel Yiu, who used to have a radio show as well as a newspaper column, said things started to change about five years ago. He thinks he had something to do with the change in attitude; he describes what he told his audience: "If a Caucasian said white people should only vote for white candidates, that would be racism. I said that if, after you've done some homework, studied the policies, and don't see much difference, you decide to vote for the Chinese, fine. But if you don't vote for any other reason, that's racism. I was criticized and attacked. But several years later, that's become the mainstream view in the Chinese-language media."

In the 2000 federal election, the Alliance candidate, Joe Peschisolido, won enough Chinese votes to defeat a Liberal cabinet minister, Raymond Chan, in Richmond. Some Chinese voters felt Chan had spent too much time travelling in his role as secretary of state for Asia-Pacific affairs and paid too little attention to constituency matters.

In 2002 Peschisolido angered many of the people who voted him in by switching his allegiance to the Liberals. They said they had voted for a party, not the obscure politician who'd carried its banner. That was significant. The Canadian Alliance has never been in power so it can't take credit for admitting any immigrants. The Richmond election showed that, in a group as large and varied as the Chinese, immigration can't always do what the Liberals expect it to: deliver seats to the Liberals.

Why would anyone expect British Columbians of Chinese ancestry to vote as a bloc in any case? No one speaks of a "Caucasian community" in which someone of Greek background is supposed to think like someone of British background. The so-called Chinese community is just as diverse. There are rich Chinese and poor, educated people and illiterates, speaking several languages that are not mutually comprehensible. Some were born in Canada; some came from mainland China, Taiwan, and Hong Kong, each a distinct society with its own political and social structure. Many of these people have nothing in common save, to a Western eye, their Asiatic features. No one person or organization could possibly speak for all of them.

If you look for a leader in the so-called "Chinese community" of British Columbia, one name keeps coming up. Lillian To is a stalwart of the immigration industry, although she wouldn't put it that way. SUCCESS, of which she is executive director, may be the most successful social service organization in Canada.

The first time I visited the SUCCESS office, some years ago, it was in an original building in old Chinatown. Since then, it has moved to a lavish new four-storey headquarters. From there, To oversees an empire that includes 11 offices, 350 employees, and 8,000 volunteers. It costs $16 million a year to operate SUCCESS, of which about $11 million comes from the government. The rest comes from its supporters. SUCCESS is the second-largest provider of language training in Vancouver. It has seniors' residences. And it offers, among other services, employment counselling, health promotion, and help for troubled families.

Lillian To knows that some people are concerned about the concentration of Chinese immigrants in parts of Greater Vancouver and is sensitive to suggestions that these new Canadians are not integrating as quickly as they should. "Most people in the Chinese community are very Canadian," she says. "What's wrong with a lot of Chinese living in Richmond close to their friends? In Richmond we have a large number of Chinese living there and we have Chinese malls, Chinese New Year celebrations, Chinese papers, and all of that. I have seen some write-ups about that being an isolated and segregated community. This is far from the truth.

"If you look at the 12-hour day of the average person, they spend most of the time working. Most people who live in Richmond don't work in Richmond; they work elsewhere and not necessarily in the Chinese community. Most are professionals. They may be working as a lawyer downtown or in sales at the Bay. Or they own their own business in Vancouver. That's at least eight hours of the day. Their kids go to Canadian public or private schools.

"So how are they segregated from the rest of the community? In their spare time, maybe they have Chinese food or watch a Chinese movie or shop in a Chinese mall? Don't English-speaking people do that? Don't they have their own friends? Don't they watch what they prefer to watch? Maybe their preference is to watch a Russian film. I am just saying that 10 to 20 percent of their time is their private time."

Ronald Leung, the talk-show host, isn't sure To reflects the views of the majority of the community, though the government assumes that she does. When a parliamentary committee came to Vancouver to gauge public opinion on immigration, it heard from a handful of official spokesmen, including To and Victor Wong, head of the Association of Vancouver Chinese-Canadians, who supported the admission of the boat migrants in 1999. "The government gives money to those organizations that work with immigrants and refugees," says Leung. "Then the government has a meeting to find out public opinion, and who goes there? The same organizations. They're all in the same business. They want more refugees. More lower-income people. More funding for more training courses. My listeners don't want those things, but they don't have time to go to meetings."

Leung has a Ph.D. in computational chemistry from Simon Fraser University. Jobs were available in the United States, but he and his wife wanted to stay in Canada. After a stint in business, he wound up in radio. He has a ready grin and a rapid-fire delivery, and he takes obvious delight in poking the pretensions of the self-appointed spokespersons for the Vancouver Chinese community.

"Our audience is educated and middle class. They are interested in education, taxes, and local and provincial politics. They seldom want to talk about federal politics, except the refugee system. They always complain about it because they came through the regular immigration process."

The local English-language media rarely carry stories about what's happening in the Chinese community, he says. Maybe if they listened to his show they'd have a better idea about what people are thinking. One day, for example, there was a hot discussion about a family living in a million-dollar house in Vancouver. The husband was back in Hong Kong working. He was sending almost no money to his wife and kids. So she applied for, and got, welfare.

Another topic guaranteed to jam up the phone lines is politics in China. Ten years ago, people were critical of the Beijing regime. Though it is still officially Communist, it is presiding

over the introduction of capitalism, and the expatriate community has become more sympathetic.

A question that often comes up when you have a large, not
fully integrated immigrant community is loyalty. What if
Canada and China were in conflict? Where would people's loyalties lie? In the aftermath of September 11, this is a raw issue.
"I know what the Chinese people would do," Leung says. "It
would depend on where their wealth is. If their relatives and
wealth were still in China, they would be pro-China. If their
wealth was now in Canada and they no longer had many friends
and relatives at home, they would be loyal to Canada. They are
very practical. A minority of them, because of their cultural
background, would be pro-China all the way. They would just
go back."

Leung used to host a show jointly with Thomas Leung,
who operates a cultural organization in Vancouver. "I asked
Thomas, 'If there is a conflict between Canada and China
sometime in the future, and you have your Canadian citizenship and you have done the citizenship ceremony and said you
are loyal to Canada, what is your loyalty?'

"He said, 'I am a Canadian citizen today but I am also a
Chinese. If there is a war, no matter what, I would go back to
China and fight for China.' I said, 'Why are you still in Canada?
You should be in China.'"

Then there's the matter of the 200,000 or so Canadian citizens from Hong Kong who have returned there because they
can make more money than they can in Canada. "We have a big
problem when those people retire and want to come to
Canada," Leung says. "We have a universal health system.
They haven't paid taxes here and they leave all their money in
Hong Kong. They don't pay much tax here. What do we do?"

As a loyal Canadian, Leung is worried by such questions.
He thinks they need to be aired. Ironically, the English-
language media shy away from them, not wanting to ruffle

ethnic sensibilities. Leung keeps his show lively by leaving the political correctness to them.

In 1993 Pushpa Seevaratnam, a doctoral student at the Ontario Institute for Studies in Education, wrote an article in the *Globe and Mail* demanding that math problems using hockey examples be removed from Canadian textbooks. She cited the case of a 10-year-old from Sri Lanka who couldn't figure out how long it would take a Bobby Hull slapshot travelling at 52.9 metres per second to travel 25 metres. Such an example was "ethnocentric," she wrote, and unfair to recent immigrants who don't know anything about hockey.

In 2002, an employee of Edmonton's largest landlord, Boardwalk Equities, slipped a note under the doorway of the apartment of Clark Barr, an 18-year-old student at the University of Alberta. The note ordered him to take down the Canadian flag fastened to the glass door of his ground-floor apartment. When he called to ask why, he was told the flag might offend non-Canadians or new immigrants. (After some embarrassing publicity, the company announced it would erect a flagpole to display the Canadian flag on the property.)

Everyone should be treated with respect and courtesy. Immigrants, struggling to adjust to a new society and a strange language, deserve special consideration. But the indoctrination of Canadians with the bizarre ideology of multiculturalism has created an odd and embarrassing phenomenon: an attitude of excessive deference towards immigrants. The Economic Council of Canada expressed its disquiet about this attitude a decade ago in its report on the economic impacts of immigration: "Some Canadians are beginning to feel they are expected to be tolerant of immigrants' different ways, but that immigrants are not required, requested, or even expected to adjust to Canadian ways. It almost seems as if Canadianism is undervalued, as if we were not proud of what our society has to offer."

The council, in its recommendations, proposed the creation of a "moral contract" outlining the responsibilities of both hosts and immigrants. This contract would be widely publicized within Canada as well as to prospective immigrants. No moral contract was ever elaborated; the proposal was denounced by the immigration industry as offensive to multiculturalism, and the government did not go near it.

The two examples above demonstrate what the Economic Council was talking about. They are the logical result of multiculturalism, a creed that seeks to devalue and eliminate anything that is distinctively Canadian. Before multiculturalism, a 10-year-old immigrant would be expected to make the Canadian obsession with hockey his own. Many, of course, did and still do; the National Hockey League is full of Canadian players whose ancestors came from all over the globe. But in multiculturalist ideology, hockey should have no special status in Canada, which is why Pushpa Seevaratnam wanted it out of Canadian textbooks.

For Boardwalk Equities, which had absorbed the same ideology, the Canadian flag had no special status. Its concern was that display of Canada's national symbol in Canada might offend an immigrant, so it ordered it removed. Of the 192 countries in the world, there is only one where such a thing could happen.

These are not mere oddities or extreme cases. The attitude permeates government, universities, and the media and extends all the way to the top of the Supreme Court. In March 2002, the court upheld a policy that gives preference to Canadian citizens for jobs in the federal public service. In doing so, it rejected the claim of three women that the policy is unconstitutional discrimination. Similar policies are common practice all over the world, one of the judges wrote, and the Canadian government has the right to "define the rights and privileges of its citizens."

The court minority, however, including Chief Justice Beverley McLachlin, appeared shocked at the idea that Canadian citizenship should have value, that it should afford those who hold it rights in Canada greater than those who do not. The majority decision, the dissenting judges declared, "violates human dignity."

The mythology underpinning immigration policy – that large-scale immigration is essential for economic growth and demographic survival – feeds into the exaggerated deference promoted by multiculturalism. Here's Royson James, a columnist in the *Toronto Star*: "If it weren't for immigration, we'd have to send out a search party around the world looking for people to keep our country afloat."

As explained in chapter 5, there is no evidence that this is true. Most other Western industrialized countries have older populations than Canada, lower fertility rates, slower population growth, and much less immigration. Yet they are doing fine without sending out search parties. Why can these countries, which appear to need immigrants more than Canada does, flourish with few of them whereas we would perish without a lot more? The only possible answer is that Canadian-born people are, in some mysterious way, uniquely deficient. Yet this deficiency is not identified.

James is not the only journalist whose arguments demean Canadian-born people for the sake of exalting immigrants. Neil Swan, the economist who headed the Economic Council study, suggested to me that Canadian attitudes to immigration issues reflect the "Calvinist Presbyterian background in this country that leads to a lot of breast-beating. It's very popular to downplay the virtues of the country." This might explain why the immigration myths and the ideology of multiculturalism have found such fertile soil in Canada. All these beliefs and ideas are based on the conviction that Canada is inadequate – culturally, economically, and in almost every other way.

In my own experience, the Canadians least likely to downplay Canada's virtues are immigrants. Unlike people born here, they chose Canada: they thought it was better than the place they were leaving or other places they might have applied to enter. Few immigrants would dream of suggesting that references to hockey be removed from textbooks or that Canadians should not have the right to display their own flag. Few would object to having to obtain citizenship before applying for a job in the public service.

Nadeem Ahmed, a computer programmer who moved to Toronto from Pakistan in 1996, told me he did not come to Canada to recreate the life of Pakistan in a sealed-off tile of the Canadian mosaic. He came because images of North America – Niagara Falls, the Rockies – that he had seen as a child thrilled him, and he wanted to be part of the place. People like Royson James seem to believe that Canada should be grateful that immigrants condescend to come here. It's an odd belief, given that an estimated 100 million people in the Third World would like to get to a Western country, and the admission tickets are hard to come by.

Ahmed does not think Canada owes anything to immigrants; he thinks it's the other way around. "For too many immigrants, the motive is all material," he says. "They come and they take and don't give back enough. They get free education, free medical care, they even get welfare if they don't have a job. What does Canada get in return? People should do volunteer work. And they should repay Canada by making the strongest possible effort to learn English.

"We Pakistanis have a separate group, the Chinese have a separate group. How long can we stay together if we can't communicate? As a whole society, we are going towards disintegration. If the country gives you a chance to better your life, it's your responsibility to pay it back. We should not take Canadian citizenship for granted as just a materialistic thing. We should be proud of being Canadian."

CHAPTER SEVEN

HOW CANADA FAILS REFUGEES

REXHIJE HAJRULLAHU AND HER FAMILY FLED KOSOVO IN 1999 with nothing but the clothes they were wearing. She was 23. The Serbian police gave her and her parents and younger brother five minutes to leave. If they weren't gone by then, they would be shot.

They ran to the railway station and boarded a train that took them close to the Macedonian border. From there, they had to walk along the tracks (not next to them, because of land mines) until they reached a muddy field. They waited 15 hours to be allowed to cross the border. Once across, they were installed in a tent in a refugee camp in an open field. It would be their home for the next two months.

Hajrullahu was trained as a nurse and an architect and spoke English. But in that miserable camp, she despaired of the future. "I couldn't stay warm and I felt sick the whole time. I just wanted to stay in the tent. I didn't want to see anybody or talk to anybody."

Fortunately for the family, some Western countries, Canada included, were selecting refugees at that camp. Hajrullahu's parents were interviewed and, the next day, saw their name on a notice board. They were going to Canada. Now they live in Calgary, where Rexhije is studying medical terminology so she can work as a medical receptionist. Neither her nursing nor her architecture credentials are accepted here, so she plans to start her education all over again. She'll study architectural engineering at the Southern Alberta Institute of Technology.

Her father, who is 61, won't go back to teaching chemistry because his English isn't up to it and he isn't trained in computers. Her mother, who used to teach grades 1 to 4, has been told she can work in a daycare. Her brother has finished high school and plans to go to college.

"At first I thought, I'm not going to make it here," she told me. "Because I didn't know anything. How do I get employed? How does the medical system work here? What do you have to do? But now, it's OK. Slowly but steadily, things are working out. The Canadians are very understanding."

I once asked Jonas Widgren, a former Swedish government official who has spent much of his life working for international migration organizations, for his definition of a refugee. He said, "A refugee is someone running for his life." A Guatemalan union leader being chased by death squads, for example. Or a supporter of democracy who'd be tortured if he fell into the clutches of a military thug like General Pinochet. Or someone who, like Rexhije Hajrullahu, is fleeing Serbs who would kill her for being Muslim.

On the face of it, Canada should be welcoming more people like Rexhije Hajrullahu as part of its refugee resettlement program. But she's not the kind of refugee the industry likes to see coming here. Because she's selected overseas by the government, she does not need a Canadian lawyer to argue her case in Canada. Nor does she need the approval of the Immigration and Refugee Board. If all Canada's refugees were like her, millions of dollars in legal aid fees would evaporate and there would be no IRB jobs for Jean Chrétien to dispense.

Canada and 140 other countries are signatories to the United Nations Convention on the Status of Refugees, the Geneva Convention. Passed in 1951, it defines a refugee as someone who's outside his or her country and can't go back because of a "well-founded fear of persecution" due to race, religion, nationality, social class, or political opinion.

Canada approves two kinds of Geneva Convention refugees. There are those who, like Hajrullahu, are plucked from among the estimated 21 million people stranded in refugee camps. In 2000, 13,566 such people came to Canada. Selected by experts who interview them in the camps, they undoubtedly fit the criteria set out by the Geneva Convention. The others select themselves by showing up at Canadian points of entry. In 2000, 34,260 self-selected claimants arrived in Canada. Most stay, either as refugees, under some other status, or as failed refugee claimants who refuse to leave. Few of them meet either Widgren's definition of a refugee or that of the Geneva Convention.

By international standards, about 15 percent of self-selected claimants are really fleeing persecution; the rest are trying to use the asylum system to move from a poor country to a rich one. Of the roughly 15 percent fleeing persecution, only a few are real refugees by the time they get to Canada. Most have already found safety in the United States or Europe and have no legitimate reason to make refugee claims in Canada.

A Sri Lankan who has reached Germany, for instance, has obtained safety from the civil war in Sri Lanka; he is no longer running for his life. If he wishes to come to Canada, he has the right to apply to the Canadian government either as a selected refugee or as a regular immigrant. But it should be unacceptable for a Sri Lankan to come uninvited from Germany to make a refugee claim, unless he can prove the Germans were persecuting him because of his race, religion, nationality, social class, or political opinion.

Under international law, Canada can send such a person back to Germany. Most other countries exercise this right; Canada chooses not to. As a result, most of those making refugee claims in Canada are not refugees but immigrants using the refugee system to cut to the front of the immigration line.

There's every reason a wealthy country such as Canada should operate a generous refugee protection program. But Canada ought not to be the place of first resort for people fleeing danger; it's too far from refugee-producing countries for that. Canada's role should be to give generous support to the United Nations High Commissioner for Refugees (UNHCR), which is charged with caring for those 21 million people, and to select the neediest among them, those least likely ever to be able to return home, and help them build new lives in Canada.

Instead, we allot most of our resources to refugee claimants who arrive at our borders and airports. Why? Because the system has been taken over by those who profit from it. It's not run for the benefit of refugees who, except for the 10,000 or so plucked from camps each year, will never see Canada. The major beneficiaries are Canadian lawyers and consultants whose livelihoods depend on a steady flow of self-selected claimants and smuggling racketeers.

Canada is one of the least generous of Western countries in the support it gives organizations charged with looking after legitimate refugees, most of whom want only decent living conditions until they can return home. We contribute about the same to the care of those 21 million refugees in camps as we pay in legal aid fees to Canadian lawyers who represent the roughly 30,000 self-selected claimants who show up at our border.

Roslyn Kunin, an economist, is executive director of the Laurier Institution, a Vancouver-based non-profit organization that supports research on issues related to Canada's cultural diversity. She would not hold that position were she not favourably disposed to immigration and multiculturalism. She was one of three pro-immigration experts chosen by the government in 1997 to conduct a review of policy. Their report, entitled *Not Just Numbers*, recommended, among other things, disbanding the IRB. It would be replaced by a new Protection Agency that would merge the functions of the IRB, which judges refugee claims made in Canada, and immigration department visa officers, who select refugees overseas. "The same criteria," said the report, "would apply in Canada and abroad."

It was a revolutionary proposal. It would mean that only Geneva Convention refugees would get Geneva Convention refugee status in Canada, which has not been the case since the creation of the IRB in 1988. Preparing the report, Kunin met with Toronto's immigration and refugee lawyers. When she told them what the commission was thinking, they were horrified. "You can't do that," one blurted out. "I have to pay for my swimming pool." As Kunin recalls, "My mouth hung open. How could a lawyer say that in a public meeting?"

She understands, of course, that many people have a considerable stake in the status quo. "It is a big system," she told me at the Laurier Institution's Vancouver office. "It's a huge hot potato. I had people look me straight in the eye and say, 'There is no such thing as a non-bona-fide refugee claimant.' These are people who work in claimant-supporting organizations. Yet virtually all the real refugees are in camps in the hellholes of the world. The people who come to Canada and claim refugee status are not in the same group."

Not Just Numbers was shelved by the Liberal government; the IRB remains intact. Meanwhile, the number of claimants rises annually. About 45,000 showed up in 2001, the most ever and a 30 percent increase over the previous year. This dramatizes the magnetic appeal of the IRB to smugglers and their clients; there is no evidence that persecution in the world increased by 30 percent during the same period.

The people-smuggling racket, estimated to be worth at least $10 billion a year, is operated by international crime syndicates. The Chinese Triads and the Russian Mafia are important players, but new criminal networks have emerged to take advantage of the fastest-growing business in organized crime. According to Pino Arlacchi, director general of the United Nations Office for Drug Control and Crime Prevention, about 200 million people are currently under the control of people-smugglers. This figure includes women sold into sexual slavery and migrants still paying off their debts to smugglers years after arriving in North America. This is a vast human tide; to put it in perspective, during four centuries of slavery, 11.5 million people were shipped out of Africa.

A typical client smuggled to Canada would be, say, a middle-class Sri Lankan Tamil. Canada is a favoured destination for Tamils for two reasons: a large Tamil community is already established here, and Canada is the only country that routinely recognizes their refugee claims. In 2000 the IRB approved 2,000 Sri Lankan claims; all other refugee-receiving countries together approved only 500.

For about $50,000, the smuggler provides a false passport and a circuitous trip around the world. There are no direct flights from Sri Lanka to Canada, so the smuggler chooses a routing through transit points where officials can be bribed to let people with dubious documents onto planes. A member of the smuggling gang recoups the false passport from the claimant during the Canada-bound flight. On arrival, the claimant says he has no documents and is a refugee.

The Canadian government abets the gangsters by releasing thousands of such undocumented, unidentified claimants each year at Canadian airports. This ensures that the criminals continue to sell Canada; if claimants were detained, Canada would be a less attractive destination and the smugglers' product would be devalued. It also allows the smugglers to sell the United States. Since the Americans usually detain undocumented arrivals, the crooks bring their U.S.-bound clients into Canada to make refugee claims. The Canadians release them and the smugglers sneak them across the border. Canada never hears from these illegal immigrants again, though the IRB uses them to make its acceptance rate less embarrassing; for statistical purposes it includes no-shows among its rejected claimants.

The government seeks to moderate the flow of refugee claimants by having officers in foreign airports check passengers' documents and stopping people with false ones from getting on Canada-bound planes. Yet it does everything it can to make Canada the most appealing place in the world to make a claim. The acceptance rate – about 60 percent of cases heard – is four times the international norm. Refugee claimants in Canada can work, collect welfare, receive free health and dental care, and get free legal assistance. Like other immigrants, they can apply for citizenship. In fact, Canada is unique in its generosity in awarding citizenship to refugee claimants; other countries take them at their word and assume they are merely seeking shelter until it is safe to go home. In Canada, most successful claimants get landed immigrant status, which allows them to remain permanently and to sponsor relatives. No other refugee-receiving country offers anything like this array of enticements. Canada should not be faulted for wanting people fleeing persecution to be well treated. But most of the claimants are not fleeing persecution.

Why does the House of Commons Standing Committee on Citizenship and Immigration not examine immigration policy to ensure that it's consistent with Canada's national interests? This Liberal-dominated committee is too busy acting as a lobby group for the immigration and refugee industry; it shows little interest in how the activities of that industry affect Canada and Canadians.

In March 2002, the committee recommended that refugees whose claims were approved get landed immigrant status, and with it the right to sponsor relatives, after only 60 days. (Currently refugees sometimes wait years before obtaining landed immigrant status.) Sixty days would allow almost no time for authorities to investigate the applicants, most of whom arrive without legitimate documents. From the standpoint of the national interest, this recommendation was insane: the refugee system is the way terrorists enter Canada. Yet six months after the attack on the United States, our politicians were seeking to make the largest and loosest immigration and refugee program in the world larger and looser. It was as if nothing had happened on September 11.

It's scandalous – not just because Canada's national security is being endangered or because people are profiting from a supposedly humanitarian program but because not enough real refugees, people who deserve protection, are getting it. In February 2000, Cesar Augusto Rodas was shot dead after being turned away by the Canadian embassy in Guatemala, where he had asked for asylum. He'd been getting death threats. In the past, the embassy in Guatemala has helped thousands of people escape death squads there and in El Salvador.

Our refugee system is overwhelmed by the ever-increasing flow of self-selected claimants. Some of them, as *Not Just Numbers* pointed out, are close relatives of people already living in Canada. They try to get in as refugees, rather than through the regular immigration program, because it is faster and because, as refugees, they can get welfare, thereby freeing their relatives of any legal obligation to support them financially.

Maybe, if the system were not so overwhelmed, the Canadian embassy in Guatemala would have helped Augusto Rodas, as it has helped others in the past. Ten years ago, a report by a Geneva-based migration organization stated: "The larger the number of non-refugees in asylum systems, the greater the risk that the genuinely persecuted will not obtain protection."

Of all the misinformation, sentimentality, and nonsense that surround our immigration system, perhaps the strangest belief is that Canada has a generous and humane system for adjudicating refugee claims. Canada's system affords little benefit to real refugees and offers every incentive to fraudulent ones, yet those who perpetuate this sordid state of affairs manage to pose as humanitarians. And they have the audacity to criticize those seeking to improve the system as being anti-refugee.

Some support the status quo because they profit from it. Others support it because they've been duped by profiteers. Who opposes it? In my experience, the fiercest opponents are those who have actually been in refugee camps. James Bissett is one. The former head of the Canadian immigration service, he's the expert on international migration issues who spent five years helping Russia set up a new immigration department. "I've been in the camps and they are dreadful, with little food and shelter," he says. "Often the camps are raided and people are raped and killed. We give the camps only between $20 million and $25 million a year. If you're a refugee in Sierra Leone, you'll get no help from us. This is an absolute disgrace."

There's a world of difference between a refugee in a camp and a person who pays $50,000 to arrive in Canada with a memorized story that his "agent" has assured him the IRB is currently accepting. Most people in the camps are women and children; in some camps, they make up 90 percent of the population. Most of those who make claims in Canada are men. "Real refugees are in the camps," Bissett says. "They are not the 35-year-old guys who have the street smarts and money to buy their way in."

Another Canadian who knows what a refugee goes through, having lived in Argentina when it was controlled by a brutal military dictatorship, is Sergio Karas, an immigration lawyer in Toronto. He came here in 1980 and 10 years later started his practice as a refugee lawyer. As a Spanish-speaker, he attracted a mainly Hispanic clientele. "I regret to say that the legitimate refugees that I represented in the early 1990s who were fleeing the death squads in El Salvador and Guatemala no longer exist in this country," he says. "Canada has lost its way, and some people want to make you believe that every Sri Lankan who pays $60,000 to come to Canada on false documentation is a refugee. I have a problem with that."

So disillusioned did Karas become that he dropped refugee work and now concentrates on cases involving skilled immigrants and temporary employees of international corporations. "The refugee system is corrupt," he says. "The way things are right now, a few lawyers and consultants benefit immensely from the system. Sometimes I read Personal Information Forms" – which refugees, usually with the help of a lawyer or immigration consultant, fill out after their arrival – "and they are nonsense – boilerplate. The refugee system is nothing but a secondary immigration stream right now."

In 60 years, Canada has gone from mindless cruelty to mindless gullibility. During World War II, Canada refused to admit Jewish refugees, sending them back to be murdered by the Nazis. The country that would not protect Jews from Nazis is now the only country that protects Jews from Jews by awarding Jewish Israeli citizens refugee status. In 2000 Canada was also alone in recognizing refugee claims by citizens of Ecuador, Chile, Grenada, Hungary, Jamaica, Kuwait, Malaysia, Poland, St. Vincent, Tanzania, and the United States.

Either these countries, most of which are democratic, are refugee-producing or they are not. Either Canada is right about them and the rest of the world is wrong, or it's the other way around. There's no evidence that the political hacks and refugee advocates on the IRB know more about the state of the world than all the decision-makers in all the other countries that admit refugees.

Perhaps the laxity of the current refugee system is an over-reaction to Canada's shameful record during the World War II period. The government of Mackenzie King was hostile to any non-white immigration and was overtly anti-Semitic. Our Commonwealth partner Australia was much more humane; it offered to accept 15,000 Jewish refugees, of whom 7,500 got to Australia. After the war, Canada finally opened its doors and admitted 186,000 displaced persons. Several waves of refugees followed, the result of political upheavals in various parts of the world. These included Hungarians, Czechs, Ugandan Asians, Chileans, and Vietnamese. Almost all were selected abroad by Canadian officials.

These refugee movements were organized ad hoc. Canada had not defined its refugee policy in legislation that distinguished refugees from other immigrants. The new Immigration Act, passed in 1976 and implemented in 1978, corrected this oversight. It incorporated the UNHCR definition of a Geneva Convention refugee, and it allowed Canada to designate special classes of refugees, such as, for example, Guatemalans who seek shelter from death squads in the Canadian embassy in Guatemala. They are not Geneva Convention refugees because they're still in their own country, but they need protection nonetheless.

This new act also established the Refugee Status Advisory Committee, whose job was to advise the immigration minister if a refugee claim made in Canada should be approved. This was Canada's refugee determination system until the *Singh* decision and the subsequent creation of the IRB. It was a system to be proud of. We understood that we were too far from refugee-producing countries to be a place to which people fleeing for their lives could come. So we went to the trouble spots and brought refugees to Canada. The United Nations awarded Canada the Nansen Medal in 1986 because, in the previous decade, we had given asylum to 150,000 people from refugee camps – more, per capita, than any other country.

The Supreme Court's *Singh* decision in 1985 and the creation of the IRB have been described in chapters 3 and 4. Some critics of Canada's refugee system have blamed the Supreme Court for the current mess. Yet the Supreme Court's view that a refugee claimant deserves an oral hearing is reasonable. If someone is going to be sent back to a situation she claims is life-threatening, she ought to be able to make her case in person to an adjudicator empowered to turn her away.

But the Supreme Court did not say Canada had to make a fool of itself by accepting 90 percent or more of refugee claims, as it did in the IRB's first years. It was the Mulroney government, not the Supreme Court, that created the IRB and staffed it with Tory party workers, refugee advocates, and refugee lawyers. And it was the Chrétien government, when Sergio Marchi was immigration minister, that appointed to the IRB Liberal variations on the patronage theme. Most important of all, it was the Mulroney government that failed to implement the "Safe Third Country" principle incorporated in the refugee legislation it passed in 1989.

Many people come to Canada to make refugee claims after they have been living safely in other countries. Such a claimant is asking one country to give him protection from persecutors in a second country. Yet he has escaped those persecutors by going to a safe third country; there is no reason why Canada should accept him. The Safe Third Country principle is fundamental to the functioning of the international asylum system. A true refugee, remember, is running for his life. He's not making an immigration decision; he's seeking protection from immediate danger. To come to Canada uninvited and make a refugee claim when you've found safety elsewhere is to abuse our system. It's called "asylum-shopping," and most countries don't allow it.

Bissett, who was in the immigration department when the post-*Singh* refugee system was being designed, knew it was going to be accommodating. "We anticipated that the Safe Third Country would protect us, so we designed a very generous refugee system," he says. "Then, three days before the enactment of the legislation, Barbara McDougall [then Tory immigration minister] announced she was not going to implement the provision. And the government never has. So we merrily go ahead now and accept everybody that comes in from Europe or the United States."

If not for McDougall's decision, Canada would not be overrun with self-selected refugee claimants who, whatever their situation before they left their homeland, had escaped danger before reaching our border. Canada could devote more energy and resources to helping refugees in camps and saving the lives of people like Augusto Rodas, the man our embassy in Guatemala turned away.

Yet McDougall had good reasons at the time. Under President Ronald Reagan, the United States was supporting odious regimes in Central America. Claimants from El Salvador and Guatemala were being turned down by the U.S. authorities. If Canada, acting on the Safe Third Country principle, turned them away at the border, they might be sent back to death in their homelands.

Canada could have designated the United States a safe third country for everybody but Salvadorans and Guatemalans, so that people from those countries would have been accepted into the Canadian refugee system while others coming from the United States were not. Joe Clark, then external affairs minister, resisted this solution because he thought it would damage relations with Washington. The Safe Third Country provision was shelved, and a refugee industry has grown up in Canada that depends on its absence.

The U.S. refugee system is less politicized than it used to be. There's no longer any reason not to consider the United States a Safe Third Country, as are the European countries from which other self-selected refugee claimants arrive. So why not enact Safe Third Country now? The Chrétien government claimed that it wanted to implement it for claimants coming from the United States but kept finding excuses not to. After September 11, a deal was said to be in the works whereby the two countries would recognize each other as safe for refugees. The United States would turn back the handful of refugee claimants who arrive there from Canada, and Canada would deny the thousands of claimants who arrive here from the United States. Later it was announced that the Americans were having second thoughts and that negotiations had bogged down. In June, as this book went to press, Canada and the

United States finally signed a preliminary Safe Third Country agreement that would allow both countries to turn back refugee claimants arriving at the Canada-U.S. border. The question was: Why had it taken so long?

Canada has every right under international law to implement the Safe Third Country principle, as it was on the verge of doing back in 1989. It never needed permission from the Americans. Canada, not the United States, decides who gets into Canada. The pretence of needing an agreement with the United States may have been an excuse not to do something that would have enraged the refugee lawyers who might be put out of business if the Safe Third Country principle were rigorously applied by Canada.

Not Just Numbers contains a concise sentence that explains why a rigorous application of the Geneva Convention is more humane than the extremely broad application that prevails in Canada: "We cannot afford to waste scarce protection resources on those who should be applying for our immigration programs."

Accurate estimates of the cost of Canada's refugee program are hard to come by, but there's no doubt it accounts for a major portion of the $4-billion-a-year cost of immigration calculated by former deputy minister Jack Manion. The $100,000 a year Canada pays an IRB member would pay the salaries of three teachers to provide education for children in a refugee camp. Which is the better use of Canada's "scarce protection resources"?

If Canada didn't approve so many unfounded claims, fewer people would make them, and we could dispense with some of the $100,000-a-year decision-makers. This won't happen until, as a first step, Canada's acceptance rate for claimants comes down from its current 60 percent to the international norm of 10 to 20 percent.

Why is Canada's rate so high? Partly because most IRB members are amateurs. They have no international experience, have never been to a refugee camp. Some have difficulty with

English and do not wish to write the detailed report required to support a negative decision. Many do not understand the fundamental distinction between persecution and discrimination.

The recent case, heard in Toronto, of a Brazilian homosexual is typical. A two-member panel heard the case in which the man asked for sanctuary as a victim of persecution because of his sexual orientation. Unquestionably there is discrimination against gays in Brazil. In 2000, to take a single example, a gay dog trainer in São Paulo was beaten to death by skinheads. But Brazil is a democratic country whose anti-discrimination laws protect sexual minorities. Brazilian society is liberal about sexual matters, and its major cities have gay districts. In short, the situation for gays in Brazil is about the same as it is in Canada or any other Western country in which gays enjoy full rights and the protection of the law but suffer from the acts of homophobes.

One of the IRB members, now retired, has a vivid recollection of the conversation that ensued when he and his colleague discussed the case in private. The retired member said, "The claimant may have suffered some discrimination, but he isn't a Geneva Convention refugee."

The other member said, "Well, my son's gay."

"So?"

"You're not sensitive to gays."

"I'm not here to be sensitive to gays. I'm here to listen to a claim, and I don't believe that this guy has suffered persecution."

Until recently, cases at the IRB were heard by two-member panels. Only one member had to accept a claim for it to be approved. So the Brazilian was classified by Canada as a refugee under the definition of the Geneva Convention. Small wonder Canada is an international laughingstock because of the IRB: other refugee tribunals would not even hear such a claim. And small wonder that the IRB, since its inception, has produced acceptance rates that astound international asylum experts.

Safe Third Country is not the only basic principle of the international asylum system ignored by Canada. Another is

"Safe Country of Origin." Any person from a country that is a signatory to the Geneva Convention and follows the rule of law is not entitled to make a refugee claim. Brazil is such a country.

Still another overlooked principle is "Internal Flight Option." If you could reach safety without leaving your own country, you have no reason to expect another country's protection. Except for the IRB, refugee tribunals around the world routinely dismiss claims from Sri Lankan Tamils, because Tamils in danger in the north can find safety elsewhere in the country; 500,000 Tamils, including the foreign minister of Sri Lanka, live in the southern capital, Colombo. Similarly, a Brazilian who finds life difficult in a small town could move almost anywhere in Brazil, including to the gay district of Rio de Janeiro or São Paulo.

The gay Brazilian is an example of a manifestly unfounded claim. Others are less obvious. Gypsies in the Czech Republic and Hungary are subjected to severe discrimination, but the discrimination is illegal, victims have recourse to the courts, and both countries are trying to improve the economic and educational status of their Gypsy minorities. For these reasons, Canada is the only country that approves refugee claims by Czech and Hungarian Gypsies. All other countries consider them victims of discrimination rather than persecution and thus not refugees.

The Czech and Hungarian governments' records in protecting the human rights of minorities are far from perfect. But so are the records of every other democratic country subject to the rule of law, including Canada and the United States. It is presumptuous and offensive for a Canadian tribunal to decide that other democratic governments are incapable of protecting the human rights of their citizens.

By approving unfounded claims, the IRB damages Canada and it hurts the entire international asylum system. Every approval strengthens the pull factor. Some people enticed out of the Third World by the IRB's approval rate are turned back trying to board Canada-bound planes at European airports, thus becoming another country's problem. In this way the allure of the IRB has the effect of clogging the international asylum system to the detriment of genuine refugees everywhere.

If the Hungarian Gypsies were running for their lives, they would go to nearby European countries. They know European countries do not accept them as refugees. They come to Canada because the IRB has shown itself willing to accept at least some Hungarian claims. Such eccentric decision-making on the part of the IRB is expensive; the *Globe and Mail* reported that in 2000 and 2001, Canada spent $64 million in processing and settlement costs on claimants from Hungary alone.

Finally, the IRB damages Canada's international relations. We insult the Czech Republic and Hungary by naming them as countries that persecute their citizens. To stop allegedly persecuted people from coming, we infuriate these countries by imposing visa requirements on all Czechs and Hungarians. A better solution would be to reform our refugee determination system.

There are many cases in which, if the claimant is telling the truth, he is undoubtedly a victim of persecution. The issue is whether he is indeed telling the truth. An IRB hearing is not a trial; a claimant does not have to prove he's telling the truth and is not cross-examined. It's up to the members to draw him out, to have him amplify his story so they can compare it with their knowledge of conditions in his home country and determine whether his story is credible.

I've met many IRB members, and the best of them, the ones who really care about refugees and are serious about their work, have low acceptance rates. They know that no Pole or American needs Canada's protection; they know that a Sri Lankan story identical to hundreds of other Sri Lankan stories they've heard is almost certainly a lie. Members with low acceptance rates (known as "strong members" within the IRB) are usually not reappointed. This is bad news for true refugees, since the strong members tend to have the greatest knowledge and the best judgment. They are the least likely to issue an unmerited positive decision, but they are also the least likely to issue a faulty negative one.

Nirmal Singh, who served on the IRB in Vancouver for 15 years before retiring in 2000, was a strong member. Despite his acceptance rate of less than 10 percent, he was reappointed, perhaps because of his Indian ethnic background; the government makes a point of demonstrating diversity among the ranks of IRB members. Singh, or "Dr. No" as some called him, worked diligently, sometimes seven days a week. Saying yes to a claimant is easy. You merely have to state that you find the claimant credible. When you say no, however, you need solid, well-argued reasons that can stand up to challenge in court. "I could say yes in the morning and yes in the afternoon, and go and play golf. I would still get the same salary," he told me. He didn't, because he took seriously his oath to be fair to claimants appearing before him and to his country.

When a pattern develops at the IRB, word spreads instantly. "Stories are made up according to whatever we want to buy," Singh says. "The word goes out: 'They're buying this. Go for it.'" A good member will challenge such stories. Singh heard some of the Chinese boat people's stories in 1999. Many claimed to be persecuted members of the Falun Gong sect but, on questioning, turned out to know nothing about Falun Gong. Having intended to sneak into the United States, they were not well prepared to make Canadian refugee claims. Singh thinks people might have got the wrong impression about the IRB when almost all of the boat people's claims were refused. There is little consistency in the IRB and whether a claim is approved depends on where, when, and by whom it is heard. "When we were finishing the boat cases, more people were coming from China wearing suits and ties and saying they'd been tortured for being Falun Gong. These cases were being approved."

What most troubles him is the disrespect for Canada and Canadians that permeates the system. "Any Canadian would give his shirt to a genuine refugee. I would invite them to my home. But when you see abuse, when you see them sitting there laughing at you . . ."

During the pro-democracy push in China that culminated in the Tiananmen Square massacre, Canada was not deporting anyone to China. Claimants would tell Singh, "Nobody's going to send us back." He recalls one claimant who said, "This hearing has no significance because you are not sending me back." Singh comments, "It was insulting – not to me, but to Canada. To every Canadian. It really shakes you up.

"We all know we'll take anyone where there is a shred of evidence that he could be in trouble. But so often, these stories are written by somebody for a few bucks and memorized. We are very generous and we could be even more generous. But all these hundreds of millions of dollars are wasted. I take it personally. Everybody's grandmother is paying taxes and they can't get into the hospital when they need it. Old people are sitting in the hall at the hospital while we accept so much abuse of the refugee system. How can we afford this luxury?"

Lubomyr Luciuk, who teaches political geography at the Royal Military College in Kingston, Ontario, is a former member of the IRB's Toronto office. What struck him about refugee claimants was the similarity of stories and the fact that no one yearned to go back home. During his visits to refugee camps, almost everyone he met wanted to go home.

Luciuk heard many Chinese claims; surprisingly, none came from anyone who opposed Communism. Most claimed they were opponents of the one-child policy or persecuted because of their Christianity. "In almost every case, religious meetings in the countryside were broken up," recalled Luciuk. "The home in which the religious meeting was held was always in a wooded area with a back door leading to a little forest on a hill. The sentries would always alert the religious people having the meeting that the Public Security Bureau was coming. Everyone would run out the back door into the woods, up the hill and, sure enough, there would be a highway with 24-hour traffic. They'd flag down a vehicle and get away."

After hearing the same story repeatedly, Luciuk couldn't help being skeptical. "If you were coming to arrest me, and there were three or four of you, wouldn't you watch the back door? Yet it was the same story every time: 'It's dark, there's woods, there's a hill, we run up, no one gets caught. And then we all end up in Canada.'"

Luciuk, too, was a strong member, but he was in a minority, and most of the dubious refugee claims based on silly stories are approved. "I don't want to paint the other IRB members as morons. In fact, some are excellent at doing the job they swore an oath to do. But some are so inclined to believe that anyone sitting there is a refugee that they seem inherently inclined to say, 'These people are telling the truth.' The vast majority of people who come before the board are liars. They're not refugees. They're economic migrants, and they're cheating us. The first lesson these people learn about coming to Canada is, 'Lie to Canadian officials – it works.' Is that a good citizenship lesson?"

Of course not. It's a bad lesson both for the people who become Canadian citizens by dint of fraud and for citizens already here. A country that allows itself systematically to be treated with contempt loses self-respect. If we don't take our refugee determination system and the gift of Canadian citizenship seriously, why should anyone else?

A refugee is someone who is running for his life. That means that if you escaped from Sri Lanka to Canada, you can't go back there even if you have pressing family business because, based on what you told the IRB, you'd be killed. You won't be able to go back to Sri Lanka until the civil war is settled once and for all.

In February 2002, when a ceasefire was reached between

the Tamil rebels and the government, it looked as if that day might be in sight. Meanwhile, Tamil refugee claimants had been streaming into Canada for years while the war was in full swing, and Canada stood by while many went back to visit. Some, a former senior official in the Canadian high commission in Colombo told me, went back even before their refugee cases had been decided. By doing so, they were admitting they had lied to the IRB by claiming they were in danger. The government can ask the IRB to revoke the status of such claimants, but it never does. By failing to pursue those who treat Canada with such blatant disregard, the government implicitly acknowledges that the refugee determination system is a farce.

Before Brian Mulroney became prime minister, Canada had an excellent system, generous by international standards and effective in helping genuine refugees. The current system largely fails to help those in need, wastes humanitarian resources, and makes a mockery of the idea of political asylum. It invites people to come here and tell lies, and it rewards them for doing so by granting them citizenship.

In the coming decade, 300,000 or so people will become landed immigrants by this method. They will sponsor long chains of relatives. And so millions of people will eventually enter Canada as self-selected immigrants, all on the basis of fraud. Our refugee system encourages criminals to carry out and expand their people-trafficking businesses. And it endangers the security of North America. After September 11, it seemed unthinkable that Canada would continue operating a refugee system that makes it easy for terrorists to get into North America. Yet here we are. The clear need for better security has been thwarted by entrenched lobbies eager to preserve the status quo.

Four changes would help minimize the security threat. First, replace the IRB with a professional tribunal composed of impartial adjudicators capable of applying the Geneva Convention as it is applied in other democratic countries that protect refugees. Second, implement the Safe Third Country principle of the international asylum system, as provided for by the Geneva Convention. Third, detain undocumented claimants. And fourth, speed up removal of terrorists, criminals, and other rejected refugee claimants.

Instead of reform, Canadians got only rhetoric from the minister, Elinor Caplan, about getting tough with people abusing the system. But she did nothing to annoy her real bosses, the lawyers who did not want the flow of claimants interrupted. As mentioned, she said that a bill already in progress was the answer to security issues raised by the terrorist attacks. In truth C-11, effectively written by refugee lawyers, would make it even harder to get rid of terrorists or anyone else.

The law contains a provision for a new layer of appeal, the Refugee Appeal Division, to which rejected claimants can appeal on the merits of their case. The government announced in April 2002 that implementation of this provision would be delayed because of an unprecedented backlog of refugee claims. Once the new system is in effect, all rejected claims will automatically be appealed within the IRB before being appealed to the Federal Court. According to IRB internal projections reported in the *Toronto Star*, this could triple the time it takes to resolve each case, from the current average of 10 months per claim to 29 months. As most claimants live on welfare, the bill will result in millions of dollars of additional welfare costs, as well as more fees for lawyers. And it will intensify the pull factor, upping the number of bogus claimants.

It's as if the Liberals aspire to make Mahmoud Mohammed Issa Mohamed the model for Canadian refugee cases. Mohamed is the Palestinian terrorist who boarded an El Al plane in Athens in 1968 and killed a passenger by shooting him in the head. The Greeks sentenced him to 17 years in jail, but he was released in 1970 as part of a deal to resolve the hijacking of a Greek plane. In 1987, he lied his way into Canada, saying he had no criminal record and had never been a terrorist. When

Canada tried to deport him, he made a refugee claim. Since then, he has appeared before the IRB 40 times, as well as in numerous court appeals. The cost of these cases is estimated at about $3 million. Mohamed is living in Brantford, Ontario; he plans to continue appealing removal orders, probably to the Supreme Court of Canada. Your tax dollars at work.

Canada must enact the Safe Third Country provision, says James Bissett, because we have organized our system in such a way that, once someone gets in, it is almost impossible to get rid of him. If Osama bin Laden wanted shelter from the wrath of the Americans, he says, the ideal place to come would be Canada. Even if our Supreme Court decided he could be extradited to the United States, Caplan's bill provides for a pre-removal risk assessment. Bin Laden would probably be allowed to stay because the United States has capital punishment.

This is the refugee system its supporters praise for its generosity and humanitarianism, and Mahmoud Mohammed Issa Mohamed is not the only undesirable to benefit from it. War criminals, drug dealers, and gang members have all used it to move to Canada permanently. They come to Canada because we make it easy to get in and easy to stay.

"There are far worse things to be than a society where immigration and refugee admissions are perceived as lax," the sociologist Morton Weinfeld, of McGill University, wrote in the *Globe and Mail* in 2001. True, but the implication – that our laxness reflects well on us, making us generous humanitarians – is outrageous. Failing to deport criminals and terrorists is not humanitarian. Approving claims by Honduran children, knowing that the next day they will be selling drugs at Vancouver SkyTrain stations, is not humanitarian. Spending millions on patent liars who spout absurd stories while spending a comparative pittance on real refugees who ask only to live in dignity until they can go home is not humanitarian.

Just as the members of the IRB seem not to understand the difference between discrimination and persecution, those who resist reform of our refugee determination system don't seem to understand the difference between generosity and stupidity. After 15 years on the IRB, Nirmal Singh understands all too well. "It's an insult to the country to be that stupid," he says. "Nobody says we're generous. They say we're stupid."

CHAPTER EIGHT

WHO GETS IN

STEVE KAUFMANN COULDN'T BELIEVE WHAT HE WAS hearing. It was as if Joe McCarthy, the Commie-hunting American senator from the 1950s, had come back to life in the guise of a Liberal MP from London, Ontario. Canada's version of McCarthy was Joe Fontana from London North Centre, chairman of the House of Commons Standing Committee on Citizenship and Immigration. In the spring of 2001, his committee held hearings across Canada to sound out public opinion prior to the passage of new immigration legislation.

As Kaufmann, a lumber exporter, found out when he attended the Vancouver hearing, neither Fontana nor anyone on the committee had much interest in gauging public opinion. The hearing was a mean-spirited exercise in bullying and thought control worthy of McCarthy at his worst. The official orthodoxy is that more immigration is better than less, and that immigration brings only benefits. Despite the compliance of much of the media in perpetuating this doctrine, most Canadians refuse to be "right-thinking" on the issue. In March

2002, for example, a Leger Marketing poll found that 54 percent thought Canada accepted too many newcomers; 26 percent thought the country was not getting enough.

But immigration does not decide elections, and the Vancouver hearing was a love-in between the politicians and the groups that support official policy and depend on government grants for their existence. Various presentations were made, including one by a group whose representative thought immigrants should be chosen on the basis of their "emotional qualities." Everybody got a careful hearing and was treated with courtesy – except for those who had the temerity to criticize immigration orthodoxy.

What reminded Kaufmann of the red-baiting McCarthy era was the treatment meted out to Dan Murray, a teacher representing the Lower Mainland Sustainable Population Group. Murray's paper was densely researched and full of the sort of information any serious parliamentary committee would be eager to absorb. He dealt with what may be the most important aspect of immigration policy, yet one ignored by the government: its impact on the environment.

Murray comes across like the serious-minded schoolteacher he is. He has worked in B.C. public schools for 25 years, the last 10 teaching ESL in Vancouver. For those who insist that critics of the immigration system must be racists and right-wingers, he presents a problem. He lives with a woman from Hong Kong. He has been active in such organizations as the Council of Canadians, Save the CBC, and Friends of Public Broadcasting. He used to be a member of the NDP.

Murray pointed out that, although it had taken 130 years for Greater Vancouver's population to reach 1.3 million, it took only another 12 years for it to climb to today's 2 million. The equivalent of the population of New Brunswick had been added to the cramped confines of Greater Vancouver in little more than a decade. Most of this growth was the result of an immigration system that marries the highest per capita intake of newcomers in the world with a concentrated settlement pattern.

Largely because of immigration, the number of cars in the Vancouver area has grown by 300,000 over those 12 years. Greater Vancouver loses 600 hectares of forested mountainside and agricultural land every year. A billion litres of waste is poured into the Strait of Georgia every year. Never taken into account when immigration policy is made is the indisputable fact that polluted air and water sicken and kill people. Under current policy, the area's population will climb to 4 million over the next 25 years. Murray cited studies by University of British Columbia scientists that prove such growth is not sustainable; it will create environmental disaster.

There was no anti-immigrant sentiment, no racism or xenophobia, in Murray's remarks. His was a straightforward presentation of facts: immigration is the major cause of the rapid, concentrated population growth that's damaging the sensitive environment of the Lower Mainland. The government's own research proves there is no demographic or economic need for so much immigration. Surely, he concluded, it's time to consider changing the policy. That the policy is unpopular, he suggested, is all the more reason to amend it. If you'd asked Vancouverites 12 years ago if they wanted the population of New Brunswick added to their region, they would have answered with a resounding no.

How did Fontana's committee react? "It was like a lynch mob," recalls Kaufmann. "Everybody had to make sure they were recorded in the minutes as being opposed to everything Dan Murray said. Fontana had just complimented everyone on the quality of their presentations, half of which were ridiculous. He said, 'I'm glad I complimented everyone before we heard from Mr. Murray.'" Later during the hearings, Murray tried to say something and Fontana shouted at him: "We don't want to hear any more from you. We know what your philosophy is."

Kaufmann found the atmosphere sinister and intimidating. "Imagine someone was testifying in the Un-American Activities

Committee and the person was a Communist or socialist and he said something socialist or Communist. However reasonable it was, he'd be pounced on." During a break, Kaufmann asked Fontana why the committee had attacked Murray. Fontana explained: "What he said was un-Canadian."

Fontana represents immigration orthodoxy, a set of views based on ignorance and opposed by a majority of the Canadian population. Murray has both solid information and public opinion on his side. Yet, according to Fontana, Murray deserves to be shouted down because his views are "un-Canadian."

If Joseph Stalin had sent a committee out to the Soviet countryside to solicit public opinion on his policy of agricultural collectivization, his committee might have operated very much like Fontana's: organized groups financed by the government would have been welcomed under the pretence that they represented the voice of the people; courageous individuals speaking up for ordinary citizens would have been sneered at, or worse.

One of the myths propounded by advocates of official policy is that those who oppose it are provincials, untutored in the ways of the world, lacking the sophistication to appreciate the benefits Canada gains from having twice as much immigration as any other country. Steve Kaufmann is hardly a provincial. Born in Czechoslovakia, he came to Montreal as a child and worked in Asia in the Canadian lumber business. He speaks nine languages, including Chinese and Japanese, and his wife, also an immigrant, is the daughter of a Chinese father and a Costa Rican mother. He's a thoughtful, experienced man whose family incarnates the ideal of multiculturalism. Yet committee members had no interest in his views.

"My three-generation family combines British-Canadian, European, Latin American, and Asian origins," he told the committee. "We are all Canadian. We have never asked anyone to 'tolerate' us or to celebrate our differences. We have just been accepted as Canadians, as individuals, without fuss." That's as it should be, he believes. Yet "official multicultural policy deals with immigrants not as individuals wishing to integrate into Canadian society but as members of ethnic collectives, disadvantaged by definition, who require special programs." That, he said, was all wrong. Why encourage newcomers to join ethnic collectives rather than become unhyphenated Canadians, as he did?

Canadian ethnicity exists: he himself is proof. Surely newcomers should be encouraged, as he had been, to embrace it as their own. This was not what the committee wanted to hear. The immigration industry thrives on the retention and strengthening of differences among Canadians. If integration replaced division as Canada's official policy, many others who appeared before Fontana's committee, employees of organizations dependent on government grants, would be out of jobs.

Another dissident no one could accuse of provincialism is Martin Collacott, a former ambassador to several Asian and Middle Eastern countries, whose wife is Vietnamese. Since retiring from the foreign service he's made himself one of the best-informed critics of immigration policy in the country. It's a subject he knows more about than anyone on Fontana's committee. The committee listened to him but cut short his presentation. Fontana then made sure Collacott got no chance to answer questions. The chairman allotted more than twice as much time to a gay and lesbian organization as he did to an articulate expert whose views, based on extensive research, challenge every aspect of immigration orthodoxy. "I don't think they listened to what either Collacott or I had to say," Kaufmann recalls. "They were there to rubber-stamp the official policy."

When Fontana got back to Ottawa in May 2001 after his "fact-finding" tour, he reported to the immigration minister, Elinor Caplan. He and his committee, he said during a session of the committee attended by the minister, found it "inspiring" to see how much support there was for government policy among people who work helping immigrants and refugees.

These people spoke "in glowing terms" of Canada's history of immigration, he assured her. "If there was one message that I thought came clear . . . it was that a lot of people said we need more immigration." He sounded like a Soviet functionary reporting back to his masters that, yes indeed, the peasants love the new collective farms.

Canada's immigration policy is in disarray because it is intellectually bankrupt. Once upon a time, when Canadian democracy was healthier, the members of an all-party committee might have tried to ameliorate this state of affairs – to think about the real issues, to challenge the minister, to analyze the impact of immigration on their constituents by looking at its influence on such quantifiable things as wages, real estate prices, the education system, and the environment.

Why is this no longer done? Partly because Parliament no longer attracts people with the intellectual weight to think for themselves or do much serious analysis. But the main reason is that politicians of all parties have bought into the notion that immigration is always beneficial and that the purpose of the policy is to satisfy the program's clients. Fontana's report to Caplan could have been summarized in two short sentences: "All is well. The clients are happy."

Fontana and the others on the committee have forgotten that they were elected to serve the people of Canada, not to act as toadies to the small group that profits from the immigration program. Despite them, the chances are good that Canadian immigration policy is going to change. There are two major reasons why this is likely to happen. First, the current policy is built on a foundation of sand. People are expected to accept the negative impact Dan Murray described so that Canada can enjoy economic prosperity and demographic survival. But, as we've seen, immigration is not necessary for prosperity, and our demographic survival is assured even if we have much less of it. The emperor has no clothes.

On the economic side, immigration makes employers and land developers and some lawyers richer, but it takes money out of the pockets of workers and it puts buying a house or renting a decent apartment out of the reach of many people. It does not create generalized prosperity; many Canadians would be better off if there were less of it.

The demographic justification is equally empty. Based on her statements as immigration minister, it is clear that Elinor Caplan was not acquainted with essential demographic facts readily obtainable in her own department's publications. She did not appear to know that immigration can do next to nothing to reduce the average age of the population. Nor that it can do little to prevent a change in the ratio of the working to the non-working population. She appeared not to grasp that immigration cannot indefinitely provide population growth in the face of below-replacement fertility. To achieve any of these demographic goals through immigration would require an astronomical intake of newcomers, one that would create a dangerous backlash among the existing population, bankrupt medicare and other social programs, and present nightmarish scenarios from environmental and urban planning perspectives.

In the absence of a resurgence of fertility, Canada's population is going to stabilize somewhere below 50 million. Should we aim immigration levels towards a stable population of 35 million? Perhaps 45 million? Should we halt the growth now? That's the sort of question a parliamentary committee that wished to make a serious contribution would be eager to study.

Immigration will determine the eventual size of the Canadian population. That alone makes it an issue of great importance to all Canadians, yet population size is never discussed. The politicians believe population growth is necessary for prosperity and that it will continue forever, despite lack of evidence. As the Organisation for Economic Co-operation and Development has shown, there is no connection between population growth and economic growth. In any case, endless population growth is a demographic impossibility.

In the absence of economic and demographic justifications, why should Canadians accept extremely high immigration levels that come with a high cost and benefit only a small minority? The politicians will be unable to ignore public opinion forever. As Canadians acquaint themselves with reliable information and attach more urgency to the questions raised by immigration, they'll force their government to stop catering to special interests and listen to what Canadians actually want.

The other reason our current program is unlikely to survive is that it poses a danger to the security of North America, danger breathtakingly realized on September 11. Canada's government may not be much concerned about security, but the Americans are; and if Canada wants its goods to flow easily across the U.S. border, it will have to allay those concerns. Immigration is now recognized, even by the Chrétien government, as a national security issue.

After September 11, the Liberals announced that security at the border would be beefed up. Eight months after the attack on the United States, the border was still undefended and Chrétien's government announced that it would remain so, despite demands from the union representing customs officers that they be armed. If armed persons seek entry to Canada, meanwhile, they are to be waved through, said a spokesman for Elinor Caplan (who, in her new post as revenue minister, is in charge of the customs service). Customs officers would then call police. Since there are no police stations next door to border points of entry, the armed intruders would probably vanish, joining the thousands of other illegal immigrants whose whereabouts are unknown to a government that seems not to take seriously its primary duty to protect citizens from harm. Sooner or later, however, Canada will be forced to do something substantive about security.

An open society can never eliminate danger, but a government attuned to the national interest, rather than to special interests, would take reasonable steps to minimize the danger. The first two steps would be to reduce the intake and to detain undocumented refugee claimants. The Americans can be criticized for many things, especially their porous southern border and their ambivalence towards illegal immigration, which many employers in the United States depend on for cheap labour. But the Americans have taken the two steps just mentioned: they detain most undocumented arrivals, and their intake, on a per capita basis, is half Canada's, even when illegal immigration is included.

Who gets in? To answer that question, we need consensus on what we want from our immigration program. To reach a consensus, we must first examine what the current program is doing to the country. That's what Dan Murray was trying to do for Joe Fontana's committee when he committed the sin of pointing out some of the undesirable consequences of the world's largest and loosest immigration program.

The goal of policy should be to maximize the benefits of immigration for all Canadians and minimize the costs. We can't minimize costs by pretending they don't exist. It doesn't happen randomly, for example, that many Canadian-born children arrive at school not speaking English and that many immigrant children are unable to learn English because it is never spoken in the schoolyard. These things are a direct result of bad immigration policy, and they can be corrected by modifying that policy.

The impacts of immigration are felt mainly in the major cities, where most immigrants live. Yet no connection is ever made between the influx of newcomers and such urban problems as poverty, housing shortages, and traffic gridlock. Greater Toronto gets almost half the immigrants to Canada. In 2000 immigration added 108,000 people to the area's population. Despite self-congratulatory talk from politicians about diversity, this influx is not particularly diverse. It would be more diverse if more immigrants were chosen by Canada and fewer were selected by the family members who sponsor them. As it stands, established communities keep getting bigger. Of the 192 countries in the world, three – China, India, and Pakistan – produced 41 percent of all immigrants to Greater Toronto in 2000.

Research published by the Canadian Council on Social Development in April 2000 documented the burgeoning poverty of recent immigrants in metropolitan areas. About 20 percent of those who arrived before 1986 lived in poverty (slightly less than the percentage of Canadian-born poor). The poverty level of immigrants who came after 1991 had soared to more than 50 percent, while the poverty level among the Canadian-born remained almost unchanged.

Why the surge in poverty among immigrants? Only 23 percent of immigrants are chosen for their occupational and linguistic skills. A proposal in the *Not Just Numbers* report to make knowledge of English or French a mandatory requirement for immigrants was ignored, so many new residents of Toronto cannot speak English. The city's employers are naturally reluctant to hire immigrants who can't communicate. The major economic impact of large-scale immigration is to drive down wages. Because almost half the immigrants come to Toronto, wage compression is felt most keenly in that city. Rapid population growth, fuelled by immigration, has driven up the price of housing; decent, affordable rental accommodation is almost non-existent. People thus have to spend too high a proportion of their income on shelter. Toronto's newspapers decry poverty and homelessness. They deplore poverty among immigrants. Yet they never make the connection to ill-managed, excessive immigration.

"Poverty rates are rising across the Greater Toronto Area," according to a report issued in 2001 by the Greater Toronto

Services Board (GTSB), an organization grouping 30 municipalities in the Greater Toronto Area. "Many people in the GTA are poorer than they were 10 years ago. There are more people living below the poverty line. The community has become unaffordable, particularly with respect to housing . . . and the lack of availability of rental housing has pushed many to live in less than optimum conditions."

This is not the fault of immigrants, most of whom arrive eager to build a better life for their families. But we have been told over and over that immigration creates prosperity and that more immigration creates more prosperity. Toronto gets close to half the immigrants who come to Canada; if immigration creates prosperity, everyone in Toronto should be rolling in money. Instead, Greater Toronto has a million people living in poverty, and poverty has increased in lockstep with immigration levels.

There is no mystery to this once one understands the economics of immigration. Suppose a Korean immigrant opens a variety store. If he works hard – and variety store owners work very hard – he can save up some money and perhaps move on to a more rewarding business. Then another Korean opens a variety store on the next block. The new store saps most of the first store's profit. There's enough business for both immigrants to survive, but neither accumulates the capital to move on to something bigger.

Who wins in this little immigration scenario? The milk company gets a cheap distribution system. Consumers get a bit more convenience. Who loses? The immigrant store owners. If there had been less immigration, if the second store hadn't opened, the original store owner might have been a winner too. Relentless immigration makes it harder for immigrants to establish themselves. That's one reason why poverty is up in Toronto; it's why the Canadian Council on Social Development found that more than half the immigrants who have arrived since 1991 live in poverty.

Immigration is responsible for 75 percent of population growth in Greater Toronto; natural increase accounts for the other 25 percent. (Migration from other parts of Canada is insignificant.) Population growth is wonderful for the real estate industry, and it benefits other sectors that are difficult for new competitors to enter: the newspaper industry, for example. If there are more people, and no new newspapers, there are more potential readers for the existing newspapers.

But population growth bestows precious little economic benefit on most people. And it harms the quality of life. "The urban area is expanding at the expense of the GTA country-side," says the GTSB report. "While the GTA contains some of the best farmland in Canada, it is mostly being replaced by new residential construction. The increase in driving and conges-tion brings a worsening air quality. If we grow too fast or we fail to plan for our growth, we will eventually be faced with more poverty, even less affordable housing, more pollution and more congestion."

Nobody in the immigration department will acknowledge the connection between immigration and poverty, or between immigration and declining quality of urban life. The GTSB report does not even mention immigration, except to say it is the main cause of population growth. How can we maximize the benefits and minimize the costs of the program if we pretend the costs don't exist?

Why does Canada have immigration? There are the official reasons, the real reasons, and the ideal reasons. Officially, we could not survive without immigration and would be foolish not to have more of it. As no evidence exists to support the offi-cial version, Canadians are supposed to accept it on faith. They're "un-Canadian" if they don't.

The real reasons Canada has immigration are that it helps the Liberal Party stay in power; it depresses wages, thereby transferring billions of dollars from workers to employers; and it benefits certain powerful industries, including the industry the program itself has created.

Ideally, why should Canada have immigration? Because many people would like to move to Canada, and because welcoming newcomers is a national tradition. But if we don't actually need immigration, the benefits should outweigh the costs. The benefits are real, but they're hard to quantify. Immigration makes the country more energetic, more dynamic, more connected to the rest of the world. The free movement of skilled workers benefits both workers and employers. The costs are equally real. They include unmanageable urban growth, poverty, wage compression, rising housing costs, and damage to the school system.

If Canada's program were based on reality rather than mythology, immigration would bring more benefits than costs. And Canadians would welcome it, not because they'd been told they need it but because they wanted it. Liberated from the straitjacket of "needing" immigration, we'd be free to have as much or as little as we want. There would no longer be any reason to accept negative consequences.

Fixing immigration does not require reinventing the wheel. Canada had a good system before Brian Mulroney and Jean Chrétien messed it up. Our own history can be used as a model for reform. And we have the example of Australia, which has shown that a battered program can be repaired. In the 1990s, the Australians, responding to abuse of their program and widespread dissatisfaction with it, reduced levels and tightened selection criteria to increase the proportion of skilled immigrants.

These changes were effected under the leadership of a minister, Philip Ruddock, the likes of whom Canada has not seen. Ruddock's philosophy, unheard of in Canada in the past two decades, is that the immigration program is run on behalf of all the people. "It is the government," he said in 1998, "not some sectional interest, that determines who shall and shall not enter this country and on what terms."

The key to reclaiming immigration from the stakeholders is to make it harder for immigrants to sponsor relatives. In Canada, working-age parents are the links that permit long chains of self-selected immigrants to enter the country. Our program has effectively been appropriated by existing communities that have the right to sponsor unlimited numbers of relatives. The Australians changed their regulations so that, in most cases, parents must be at least 65 to come as sponsored relatives. Canada should do the same, either by changing its rules or by putting a quota on the number of unskilled working-age parents it will admit each year. Such a step would require a change of attitude whereby Canada's interests are given priority over the demands of immigrants. This can't happen as long as the government believes it has a moral obligation to reunify extended families that have separated voluntarily.

The Australian position is that if family reunification is important to someone who has moved to Australia, it can best be achieved by that person returning home. When the regulation was changed, Ruddock went to ethnic organizations and asked immigrants, "Why do you want your parents here anyway?" It turned out that many were just as happy not to have them.

This change would disappoint some immigrants, but it would benefit Canada in two ways. First, we could have a higher proportion of skilled immigrants. Today, fewer than a quarter of immigrants are assessed under the points system, versus about a third in 1971. And while the proportion of unskilled immigrants was rising, good jobs for unskilled workers were disappearing. Does Canada want an advanced, high-tech economy or a sweatshop economy? If the former, then at least 40 percent of all individuals admitted ought to be chosen for their education and linguistic skills.

The second reason for cutting down on sponsorship is to produce a more diverse intake. This will happen only if existing immigrant communities are able to sponsor fewer people. Why should 55 percent of all Canada's immigrants come from only 10 countries? If diversity is a goal of our program, we must diversify the intake. The way to do that is to increase selection and reduce sponsorship.

To make immigration fully responsive to Canada's needs, we need to free ourselves from the weird idea that Canada should aim for an annual level equal to 1 percent of the population. Why is this the country's official goal? Because it was included in the Liberals' Red Book of campaign promises for the 1993 federal election. The Red Book stated that 1 percent had been the level for more than a decade, but this was untrue. An intake of 1 percent had been reached only once in the years between 1960 and 1993. The average intake was 0.63 percent, and most years it was about 0.5 percent. Our official immigration target, in other words, appears to be based on the inability of Liberal workers, putting together the 1993 election platform, to use the percentage function on a calculator.

One percent does not sound like a big number, but as an immigration level it is huge. No other country contemplates anything like it. Canada's policy on levels is as incomprehensible, by international standards, as its refugee policy. We are not going to run out of people. The average age of Canadians is increasing because of lower fertility and longer lifespans. This is happening everywhere in the world, and the process is further advanced in Europe. Only in Canada, which has the world's most powerful immigration lobby, is this universal demographic reality portrayed as a crisis to be remedied through immigration.

Aging has its bright side, as Marcel Mérette of the University of Ottawa has shown. In Europe investments in human capital (education and training) that accompanied aging in seven industrialized countries increased economic growth more than it would have increased in the absence of aging. The same will happen in Canada, unless a policy that swamps the country with cheap labour is seen as a substitute for investment in human capital.

Proponents of levels of 1 percent or higher have never explained why only Canada, of all the countries in the industrialized world, needs so much immigration. People in other countries can prosper without massive immigration; why can't Canadians?

The rest of the world understands, in a way that Canada seems not to, that immigration is not a quick fix for low fertility. When the population grows because of natural increase, growth is spread across the country. Growth through immigration is confined to the big cities. Canada's geographic size, therefore, is irrelevant to immigration.

It's been suggested that, as a solution to population losses in have-not regions, immigrants should be dispersed. The idea is unrealistic. Immigrants will go to places like Cape Breton and rural Saskatchewan only when other Canadians do: when it's possible to prosper in such places. The idea of requiring immigrants to live in a certain place as a condition of entry is repugnant, for it would create a group of second-class citizens. Besides, freedom of movement is a basic freedom to which immigrants have the same right as everyone else.

In 2000 the three biggest Canadian cities attracted 75 percent of all immigrants. This is too many people for these cities to accommodate. Most of the disadvantages of immigration – exploited sweatshop labour, language problems in schools, rising poverty levels among immigrants, housing shortages, traffic gridlock – are attributable to these excessive numbers.

When Canada had a rational program, annual numbers fluctuated according to economic and labour market conditions. Nobody but the immigration department paid any attention when the intake declined from 121,000 in 1982 to 89,000 in 1983, a 25 percent drop. Today anyone arguing for a 25 percent drop in levels would be accused of harbouring ill will towards immigrants, perhaps of being a racist. It's an infantile notion, like saying that someone who eats two helpings of ice cream is anti-ice-cream because he doesn't finish the whole carton.

In fact, to call for reasonable immigration levels is to be pro-immigration. Lower numbers minimize the negative impacts of immigration; high ones maximize the costs. Immigration works better when the numbers are more manageable. The typical annual intake since World War II is 0.5 percent. That is about 150,000. The demographer Roderic Beaujot assures us that a level of 200,000 will guarantee no decline in Canada's labour force. A fluctuating level somewhere between those two numbers, with 200,000 as a ceiling, not a target, would be generous. And Canada would remain the largest receiver of immigrants in the world.

When the country needed bodies to till the soil on the prairies, we opened the gates wide to immigrants. A huge influx arrived between 1902 and 1914, and the memory of that remarkable period is one reason people think of Canada as a nation of immigrants. But that memory has had a harmful legacy; it has led many Canadians to view immigration as a quick fix for other problems.

It's no coincidence that European countries with no large-scale immigration have developed excellent child care and early childhood education programs. Canada chose immigration to address the child-care issue, importing thousands of women from the Caribbean and the Philippines to work as nannies. Few of these women, diligent and delightful as so many of them are, could provide kids with the kind of head start, intellectually and linguistically, that trained professionals can. In Europe the systems are available to all citizens; here only the relatively wealthy can afford a nanny. And our child-care jobs are not well paid, which leaves many of these women in poverty.

Most European countries, lacking large-scale immigration, have apprenticeship systems. Canada doesn't. To judge from the statements of some employers, you'd almost think the rest of the world has a duty to supply Canada with skilled workers.

It doesn't, and it won't. Canada needs to develop systems to train its own workers. Immigration cannot provide a quick fix for all our inadequacies.

The chief shortcoming of our program is that it is expected to achieve things it can't possibly achieve. It is not a fix for low fertility or for skilled labour shortages. It can't make the population younger. It can't make the population grow forever. It can't make the economy boom, and it can't make the average citizen wealthier.

But it can provide a burst of vital energy. It can provide a haven for true refugees. It can supply some skilled workers, giving Canada a modest brain gain to counteract the brain drain to the United States. And, properly managed, it can give us cultural richness and diversity.

Who gets in? Let's not answer that question without using all the tools and information available to us. Let's not answer on the basis of emotionalism and rhetoric, or on behalf of entrenched interests. We need to scale down the size of the immigration program and our expectations of what it can do for us. We need to liberate ourselves from the flawed policy that our government and its clients tell us we need. It's time to devise more modest, more realistic, and less hypocritical immigration and refugee policies. It's time to return the immigration program to its rightful owners: the Canadian people.

NOTE ON SOURCES

THE BEST WAY TO KEEP UP WITH IMMIGRATION TRENDS and events, in Canada and around the world, is through the superb news service of the Center for Immigration Studies (www.cis.org), a non-profit research organization based in Washington, D.C. Everything that appears online about immigration is available from CIS, including news articles and opinion pieces from every perspective.

It is not possible to understand immigration policy and its impact on people without reading *Heaven's Door: Immigration Policy and the American Economy*, by George Borjas (Princeton University Press, 1999), available in paperback. Although the book is mainly about the United States, Borjas's analysis is equally applicable to Canada. (Unfortunately, outdated data lead him to overstate the amount of skilled immigration in Canada.)

The formula devised by Borjas to estimate the immigration surplus in any free-market economy is as follows: immigration surplus as a fraction of GDP = 0.5 × (labour's share of national income) × (percentage drop in native wage due to immigration)

× (fraction of labour force that is foreign-born). Borjas's calculation of percentage drop in the native wage due to immigration is based on the work of Daniel Hamermesh (*Labor Demand*, Princeton University Press, 1993), who examined the responsiveness of wages to changes in supply. In the case of Canada, a 17 percent increase in supply, due to immigration, reduces wages by 5 percent.

For those who want to know more about the relationship between economics and Canadian immigration policy, an excellent place to start is an academic paper, *The Economic Goals of Canada's Immigration Policy, Past and Present*, by Alan G. Green and David A. Green (1996). It can be downloaded from the Web site of Research on Immigration and Integration in the Metropolis (www.sfu.ca/riim). An older but more thorough and still very useful study is *Economic and Social Impacts of Immigration* (1991), by the Economic Council of Canada.

For the relationship between immigration and demographics, see *Immigration and Canadian Demographics: State of the Research* (1998), by Roderic Beaujot. It is published by the Strategic Policy, Planning and Research division of Citizenship and Immigration Canada and is available on its Web site (www.cic.gc.ca). Also available on the Internet is *The Bright Side: A Positive View on the Economics of Aging*, by Marcel Mérette, a paper published in 2002 by the Institute for Research on Public Policy (www.irpp.org).

Especially useful on the subject of multiculturalism are Neil Bissoondath's *Selling Illusions: The Cult of Multiculturalism in Canada* (Penguin, 1994) and *The Illusion of Difference: Realities of Ethnicity in Canada and the United States*, by Jeffrey Reitz and Raymond Breton (C.D. Howe Institute, 1994). Multiculturalism, as well as immigration and refugee policy, is cogently analyzed by Martin Loney in *The Pursuit of Division: Race, Gender, and Preferential Hiring in Canada* (McGill-Queen's University Press, 1998). For an account of the beginnings of multiculturalism policy, see Richard Gwyn's *Nationalism Without Walls: The*

NOTE ON SOURCES

Unbearable Lightness of Being Canadian (McClelland and Stewart, 1995), which also contains an excellent overview of immigration policy.

For the history of Canadian immigration policy, see *Critical Years in Immigration: Canada and Australia Compared*, by Freda Hawkins (McGill-Queen's University Press, 1989). The story of the peopling of the west is vividly told in Pierre Berton's *The Promised Land: Settling the West 1896-1914* (Penguin, 1990). For a detailed account of the political bungling that has left Canada's immigration program in its current woeful state, see Charles Campbell's *Betrayal and Deceit: The Politics of Canadian Immigration* (Jasmine Books, 2000).

Two recent papers will provide the reader with more detail on Canadian refugee policy. They are *Terrorism, Refugees and Homeland Security*, by Martin Collacott (Distinguished Speakers Series in Political Geography, Royal Military College, 2002), and *Canada's Dysfunctional Refugee Policy: A Realist Case for Reform*, by Stephen Gallagher (Canadian Institute of International Affairs, 2001).

INDEX

INDEX

INDEX

The text in this book is set in Janson, a typeface named for the
Dutch printer Anton Janson but based on 17th-century
original types cut by Miklós Kis. It was adapted for the
Linotype machine in 1952 by Hermann Zapf.

Book design by Blaine Herrmann